REVELATIONS

R E V E L A T I O N S

Alabama's Visionary Folk Artists

Text by Kathy Kemp
Photographs by Keith Boyer

Introduction by Gail Trechsel

CRANE HILL
P U B L I S H E R S
Birmingham, Alabama
1994

Published by

CRANE HILL
PUBLISHERS

2923 Crescent Avenue
Birmingham, Alabama 35209

Front cover painting, *Ezekiel Visions #2*, 1993, by Myrtice West.
Oil on canvas. Dimensions: 42" x 45".
Courtesy of Marcia Weber / Art Objects, Montgomery, Alabama.
Back cover painting, *Jesus is the Answer*, ca. 1985, by Reverend Ben Perkins.
Acrylic on cardboard, wood frame. Dimensions: 44" x 35".
Courtesy of Robert Cargo Folk Art Gallery, Tuscaloosa, Alabama.

First edition, first printing, June 1994.

Library of Congress Cataloging-in-Publication Data

Kemp, Kathy, 1954-
    Revelations : Alabama's visionary artists / text by Kathy Kemp;
photographs by Keith Boyer; introduction by Gail Trechsel.
        p.   cm.
    Includes bibliographical references.
    ISBN 1–881548–07–4 : $60.00
    1. Outsider art–Alabama–History–20th century. 2. Assemblage
(Art)–Alabama.   3. Garden ornaments and furniture–Alabama.
4. Artists–Alabama–Biography–History and criticism.   I. Boyer,
Keith, 1957-   . II. Title.
N6530.A2K46   1994
745' .0976––dc20   94–6943
                                                                                          CIP

Works of art pictured in this book have been credited to their owners
at the time the photographs were taken.

Printed in Singapore

For Louie D. Kemp, my Daddy. – KK –

For my wife, Cindy, whose love and support helped make this book possible.
And to the artists, whose work and vision have been an inspiration. – KB –

TABLE OF CONTENTS

PREFACE

n 1984, several years after I joined the staff of the *Birmingham Post-Herald*, I drove across town, up a hill behind the airport, down a driveway leading through a maze of rusted cars and discarded furniture, to a house belonging to Lonnie Holley.

I was there to do a profile of Holley. A former cook, he had become known to local schoolchildren as "The Sand Man" for the sculptures he carved from industrial sandstone. Expecting to meet a simple man, I left several hours later, reeling from the complexity of both Holley and his art. He talked about his life, but mostly he spoke of God, who not only had blessed him with a miraculous ability to carve, but also had seen fit to ignite in him a passionate desire to create.

Before I left, Lonnie picked up a piece of black sandstone and carved an Indian, complete with headdress, and handed it to me as a gift. It still occupies a special place in my living room.

Holley was, for me, a revelation–of both talent and humanity. In a three-hour visit, by simply being himself, he was able to change my ideas about art and people.

A couple of years passed before I met anyone else like Lonnie Holley. In 1986, I drove to Summerville, Georgia, to

Surrounded by a maze of artwork made from salvaged junk, Lonnie Holley, with two of his five children, works on a new piece under the shade of the trees in his yard near the Birmingham International Airport.

PREFACE

interview the Reverend Howard Finster, an Alabama native and folk art superstar. Like Holley, he had created, from junk, an amazing art environment outside his home. He, too, spoke of God's wondrous gift of art and his own compulsion to create.

Many of Finster's paintings were inspired by the Bible, especially the Book of Revelation. Yet while he held strong views about what constituted sin, Finster welcomed visitors with love, and not judgment.

During the next eight years, with help from my friend Robley Hood, I sought out and reported on other uniquely creative people, including Fred Webster, the Reverend Benjamin Perkins, Charlie Lucas, Nora Ezell, Mose Tolliver, Jimmy Lee Sudduth, W. C. Rice, Woodie Long, Virgil Perry, and Myrtice West. So much more than merely self-taught artists, they were, without exception, fascinating and inspiring people.

Keith Boyer, who worked at the *Post-Herald* for a number of years, took the photographs that ran with my 1986 newspaper story on Howard Finster. By the early 1990s, when he was starting to collect antiques and do his own woodcarvings, Keith shared my enthusiasm for Alabama's visionary folk artists.

From our many discussions on the art and artists grew the idea for this book. We decided to focus on artists who were born in and grew up in Alabama, or had lived a significant portion of their lives here. Our goal from the beginning was to present the artists just as they are, without the highfalutin analysis and interpretation that so often fill books such as this.

We wanted the art to speak for itself, and we decided that was also a good way to present the artists. Yet we did need the wisdom and guidance of an art expert. So we sought out Gail Trechsel, of the Birmingham Museum of Art, who had often helped me with my newspaper reports. Besides writing the introduction for this book, she offered guidance in selecting the artists and choosing the finest examples of their art. To our busy friend Gail, we are especially grateful.

There are many others who helped with this project—providing information, loaning art, proofreading the manuscript, and just lending important moral support. They include: Kay Argo, Bill Arnett, Jack and Margaret Black, Cindy Boyer, Joey Brackner, Jeff Brown, Pepper Brown, Theresa and Fred

Howard Finster's World's Folk Art Church *towers over his two-acre homemade park known as Paradise Garden in Summerville, Georgia. The garden consists of a maze of found-object sculpture and environmental art.*

10

REVELATIONS

Buchanan, Robert Cargo, Georgine and Jack Clarke, Steve Cleyton, Susann Craig, John Denton, Diane Derzis, Miriam Fowler, Kurt Gitter, Anton Haardt, Peggy Hilyer, Robley M. Hood, Lynne Ingram, Drucilla Kemp, Michael Leondas

Kirkland, Kyle Kirkwood, Dot Long, Virginia Martin, Percy Marino, Tut Riddick, Paul Ritchelson, Rena Selfe, Karim Shamsi-Basha, Margaret Traylor Staffney, Phyllis Stigliano, Micki Beth Stiller, Haydn Trechsel, Steve Warren, Marcia Weber, Marvin White, and Alice Yelen.

Also, the Alabama Decorative Arts Survey; Alabama State Council on the Arts; Birmingham Museum of Art; Birmingham Civil Rights Institute; Birmingham Jazz Hall of Fame; Clary Sage Gallery; Fayette Art Museum; Fine Arts Museum of the South; Kentuck Museum; Luise Ross Gallery; Museum of American Folk Art; Rising Fawn Folk Art Gallery; the Tartt Gallery; and the *Birmingham Post-Herald* staff, especially Jimmy Denley, Jim Willis, and Suzanne Kennemer Dent.

We also are grateful to our publishers and fellow folk art collectors Ellen Sullivan, Bob Weathers, and the rest of the staff at Crane Hill.

Most of all, we thank the artists. Meeting them, seeing their work, and hearing their stories has been a joy. We see this, their book, as a collection of revelations, in every sense of the word.

Kathy Kemp
Birmingham, Alabama   January 31, 1994

11

On the property of Annie and Charlie Lucas in Autauga County, Alabama, stands one of Charlie Lucas's large metal sculptures, made of found objects and salvaged junk.

ALABAMA: FERTILE GROUND FOR THE SELF-TAUGHT VISIONARY

GAIL TRECHSEL

had lived in Alabama only a few months in 1977, when friends took me to see Jimmy Lee Sudduth. The excursion took us more than two hours west of Birmingham through a rural, coal mining landscape to Fayette, Jimmy Lee's hometown. The artist's canvases were boards, metal barrel tops, and other salvaged objects. He painted with mud mixed with a little sugar, and derived his colors from the natural variation in the clays or plant materials at hand.

At the time, Sudduth was best known for the pictures of log cabins he frequently displayed at festivals and art shows. But he had produced an impressive range of images—from portraits of friends and celebrities, to buildings, animals, and vehicles. Not long after my afternoon at Sudduth's house, I met Mose Tolliver and Lonnie Holley, and my appreciation for the refreshingly original work of these self-taught Alabama artists began to grow—as did my appreciation for the environment that produced and nourished their distinctive personal visions. I wasn't alone in my appreciation.

During the 1970s, public interest in paintings and sculptures by artists such as Sudduth, Tolliver, and Holley, who had not been trained in formal art schools, began to grow. Some collectors and curators began to dub them "outsiders" because these artists' sensibilities seemed to come from a private,

external source—unconnected to previously known schools. Although many formally trained artists, collectors, and museums had been accumulating and exhibiting what was called folk, naive, or popular art since the early twentieth century, widespread appreciation remained limited. In the past fifteen years, however, interest has broadened with an enthusiastic audience enjoying these works not just in museums and galleries, but on album covers and tee-shirts, and on the frenzied buying battlefield of the folk festivals.

By the 1980s, art had become big business, and the romance of the isolated, solitary artist driven to create, unmotivated by money and fame, began to have a great appeal. The images of the self-taught, sometimes humorous, sometimes startling in their honesty, attracted people tired of the theoretical in studio art production. The use of humbler materials, including found and recycled objects, was a refreshing contrast to the glitz of the 1980s art market. Artists not trained by art schools revived the spirit of anti-elitism that runs deep in American culture. The poetry and spirituality in much of their work appealed to a society searching for its soul.

The aesthetic appeal of this work cannot be specifically identified, but in general it springs from the boldness and expressiveness of the images, the innovative approach the

13

INTRODUCTION

artist takes with the subject and materials, and the absolutely original and non-derivative nature of the art. The art is wrought with such a self-confidence that it captures the viewer's sensibility and imparts a truth and authenticity many viewers feel is missing from contemporary art.

Much of self-taught art is narrative and autobiographical, expressing profound truths in a direct and powerful manner. Ironically, in depicting their personal experiences of religion and grace, love and honor, suffering and pain, these artists who are defined as rural isolates and "outsiders" create universal messages that reach across all levels of society. Their truths transcend the personal by providing windows onto a set of experiences or values that illuminate life in surprising or unconventional ways.

Lonnie Holley turns a discarded television screen, some wire, and cloth into a message about communication and children. Charlie Lucas assembles castoff materials, including a desk lamp, to honor his ancestors and "turn the light on" his family and their art. Lucas says he is "after the true meaning of me," and each piece of art he creates is a means to that end. Finding a purpose for thrown-away materials extends to himself as he finds a constructive purpose for his own life.

In the art world we struggle to find the right name or label for this art—a word or phrase that will easily identify it. Folk, naive, self-taught, vernacular, and outsider are but a few attempts at classification. Still it eludes categorization, and as the twentieth century draws to an end, we appear to be no closer

Jimmy Lee Sudduth's Seven People Walking, *1985.*
Mud and house paint on board. Dimensions: 15" x 27½".
Robert Cargo Folk Art Gallery, Tuscaloosa, Alabama.

to an easy definition for this work. Yet, we are much closer to understanding it. There is a greater respect today for the variability of the arts; people are more comfortable making distinctions without being categorical or hierarchical. And, as more formally trained artists borrow from and are influenced by the work of the self-taught, categories are beginning to erode, in both exhibitions and criticisms.

Additionally, as works by several, then dozens, now hundreds of visionary folk artists are assembled, it becomes apparent that something bigger is going on. Art historians are begin-

ning to view this work in a broader context and compare it to art of this century made by both trained and untrained artists. The art of the visionary or self-taught can no longer be seen as separate and tangential, but rather as a full-scale movement within the history of art.

The authors of this book chose the term "visionary folk art" to describe the artists included here. A visionary is defined in the Oxford English Dictionary as one who is "capable of receiving impressions and obtaining knowledge by means of visions." Some of these artists, such as Howard Finster, Juanita

A small wooden chapel, decorated with crosses and messages, stands among the thousands of crosses that cover the property of W. C. Rice in Prattville, Alabama.

Rogers, and Gertrude Morgan, say they were called to make art by visionary apparitions or otherworldly voices.

Even without the literal experience of a visitation or an otherworldly vision, however, the work of the artists included here is driven by emotion, intuition, obsession, and fantasy—more so than the work of most formally trained artists. The work here comes from an extremely personal, not theoretical, motivation. This also differs from the motivation of the traditional folk artist—the basket maker or potter or quilter—who is working within the structure of a community, who learns in a master-apprentice relationship, producing within parameters that govern, even if loosely, how materials and techniques are used. Not so with the self-taught visionary, whose work knows no rules except those imposed by the vision from within.

Also important to the authors of this book is the question of why the Alabama environment has nurtured so many of these artists. Although work of this type is found all over the world, there is a substantial number of artists working in Alabama. This concentration of visionary folk artists may be explained by the distinctive culture of the South.

Much of Alabama is still rural, with small populations outside the few larger metropolitan centers. These artists are not isolated in the sense of being cut off from any contact; in fact most are well connected to their geographical and cultural roots. They have telephones, televisions, and receive junk mail. But many are isolated from the larger community in the sense that they are free from some of society's rules and conventions.

Layered onto this scenario is the important role that religion plays in everyday life. The emphasis on an established religious practice is typically greater in the South than in other areas of the country. More people here go to church, read the Bible, and hold fundamentalist views of Biblical scripture.

This life-size "castle," built by Billy Clemmons in Florence, Alabama, represents one example of environmental art in Alabama. It is shown here after partial demolition by a local church group. Photo courtesy of Wayne Sides.

Accordingly, religious messages are more freely expressed. This is evident in the work of many visionary artists including Myrtice West, Benjamin Perkins, and Howard Finster. They are able to use their art as a way of preaching the gospel and spreading the word.

In addition, there may be a greater compassion and understanding in Alabama and in the South for the eccentric; for the person expressing his or her own values–religious or otherwise–in unconventional ways.

Maybe it's the billboard on Interstate 65, emblazoned with the devil surrounded by flames, and the words "Go to CHURCH or the Devil will get you"; maybe it's the neighbor's decorated yard, filled with a variety of plants and objects including birdbaths, tires, concrete statues, and washtubs; maybe it's the garage covered with license plates, hub caps, and trade signs. Through these and other examples we are conditioned to accept and appreciate the art objects and art environments created in Alabama by her visionary artists.

As writer and critic Tom Patterson stated in *Outsider Artists in Alabama*:

"Whereas in many cultures the kinds of obsessive creativity exhibited by these artists might tend to be seen as signs of madness, in the South–and particularly in its rural areas–they're more likely to be regarded as demonstrators of intense religious faith, signs of prophecy, or evidence that artists are somehow 'touched' by God and therefore deserving of special respect (or even 'touched by the devil' and therefore best left alone)."

One of the earliest examples of individual expression in Alabama can still be seen in an environmental garden known

The Ave Maria Grotto, *on the grounds of St. Bernard Abbey, Cullman, Alabama, consists of 125 small stone and cement structures. The grotto, built into a landscaped hillside, is the handiwork of the late Brother Joseph Zoettel, O.S.B., a monk of St. Bernard Abbey for almost 70 years.*

17

as the Ave Maria Grotto, located in Cullman. The grotto is on the grounds of St. Bernard Abbey, which was founded in 1891. It consists of a hillside filled with 125 small stone and cement structures, elaborated with shells, glass, cold cream jars, and other materials, created in the early twentieth century by Brother Joseph Zoettel, a Benedictine monk at the abbey. As one of Alabama's major tourist attractions, it has for decades contributed to the way the public understands the cultural landscape.

Several of the artists in this book have developed extensive gardens or art environments of their own. Most notable are Howard Finster, Benjamin Perkins, Lonnie Holley, and Charlie Lucas. Their environments offer a greater forum for expression and are an extension of their art making. The work can and does stand alone, but the environments amplify it and give it a greater resonance. Seeing the art of these visionaries in the context of their environments, where it is made and "exhibited," strengthens the viewer's appreciation. The connection between the maker and the space can be crucial to the meaning and thus to the understanding of the work.

For environmental artists such as W.C. Rice, and for other Alabamians not included in this survey, such as George Kornegay, Billy Clemmons, and West Latham, the environment is the entire focus, with little or no desire to make or sell works separately.

The surrounding community is not always tolerant of visionary outdoor expression, but on the whole, there is a growing awareness of these environments and their special value, if not sacredness, to the communities in which they are located. Many towns and cities across the country have cooperated in protecting some of these unique personal spaces. One of the oldest organizations devoted exclusively to preserving environmental art in its original context is S.P.A.C.E.S., which stands for Saving and Preserving Arts and Cultural Environments. This group's most notable achievement to date has been to save Los Angeles's celebrated outsider installation, Watts Towers.

Today we are at an important crossroads regarding the work of visionary artists. There is regret mixed with pleasure. Pleasure in the financial success achieved by some of these artists, and in the work's appreciation and acceptance by a broader audience, and regret over the changes wrought by the marketplace. Artists are often pressured into producing numerous works with the same theme or subject matter, regardless of the harm this does to the creator, as well as the direction, character, and integrity of his art. There is the concern, too, about the way visionary artists are compensated for their work. As Alabama State Council on the Arts folklorist Joey Brackner has noted, given the appropriation by trained artists of outsider art, soon the only difference between the two groups will be socioeconomic.

As the distance between the previously separate worlds of artist and market narrow, there is the fear that the uniqueness and power of the work will be diminished. As it becomes more of a commodity, its spirituality is weakened.

There is no question that, as the popularity of visionary folk art continues to accelerate, profound changes are occurring. While concern over these changes may seem overprotective, controlling, or even patronizing, it stems from a deep respect for the art and the artists, and for what they offer. As writer Roger Manley has said, these artists give us something we need. They keep away the sameness and provide an antidote to increasing homogenization. They give us the tickets to our blue highways. As respect for them grows, let us hope their contributions to the history of art are strengthened by our appreciation.

LLOYD "BUZZ" BUSBY

**Born June 10, 1906, in Calera, Alabama
Died May 13, 1992, in Calera**

Always smiling and eager to meet a new friend, Lloyd "Buzz" Busby welcomed a growing number of visitors to his home in Calera, Alabama, in the 1970s. Many were strangers curious about the friendly army of wooden figurines that decorated Busby's yard.

Some of the figurines were farm animals, stuck in the ground with metal spikes attached to the bottom of a plywood base. But the ones that attracted the most attention were Busby's little wooden people, dressed in ragtag clothing, posing in family-size groups all over his property.

"He had quite a few people come by and buy his pieces," says Busby's daughter, Peggy Hilyer. "There was a doctor from Shreveport, and also a gentleman from Washington, D.C.

"Daddy always referred to it as junk. But sometimes these people would come buy one hundred fifty dollars worth of dolls and things from him, which would just fascinate him. Because to him, it was just something he was doing to have fun."

Busby began creating his wooden people in the early 1970s, after he'd retired from a long career as a construction worker and carpenter. Yet he had been making things for years, says his daughter, who lives near Greenville, South Carolina.

She recalls an old photograph, taken when her father was just a boy. In it, he has one finger heavily bandaged, the result of a miscalculation in his early woodcarving.

"His hobby was always woodworking," Mrs. Hilyer says. "In the early days he'd make windmills and those wooden animals to go in the yard. At first he worked from patterns, but as time went on, he created his own designs. And it got to the point where he wouldn't waste anything.

He was bad about picking up things he'd see and then using them in his woodwork."

Busby spent most of his life in rural Calera, where he grew up—"barefoot and in short pants," as his daughter recalls—with his six brothers and sisters. He attended local public schools and then, as a young man, headed to Havana, Florida, to work in a sawmill owned by his brother-in-law.

There, in 1927, Busby married the woman who would remain his wife for more than 60 years. They returned to Alabama and settled down on a little farm in Calera, where they raised four children. Busby worked construction during the day and helped his hired hands on the farm when he got home in the afternoons.

Photo courtesy The Tartt Gallery.

20

Skeet Ozley, *1986.*
Mixed media on wood. Dimensions: 49" h.
Collection of Micki Beth Stiller.

By the time his children came along, Busby was proficient enough at his hobby to make them all kinds of toys. He built his son little wooden trucks and cars. And he gave his girls a Christmas they would never forget.

"I can remember just like it was yesterday," Mrs. Hilyer says. "My younger sister and I wanted doll beds that Christmas, and he made them. I can remember they were painted pink and blue. Our mother made the mattresses and pillows for them. And they were nicer than anything you'd buy in the stores."

The family eventually left the farm and moved closer to town, where their house was a happy weekend gathering spot for any number of friends and relatives. Busby's wife, Ollie Mae, was famous for her cooking. And Busby delighted visitors, especially children, with his woodworking talent.

In his home workshop filled with nearly every tool imaginable, he made many useful items, including gun cases and racks and children's swings. Not long after his retirement in 1971, Busby began to create fewer utilitarian pieces and concentrate on those that entertained him.

His plywood people, some almost life-size, soon began to appear on his lawn in scenes he carefully arranged. As his daughter recalls, Busby would first pencil the figures on plywood, cut them out with a jigsaw, and then finish them with paint. He positioned some of his little people on the patio and others near the creek that ran by the house.

Busby named most of his characters after friends and relatives and dressed many in outfits his wife provided. Construction workers, wearing little hard hats, seemed to predominate his crowds of wooden people.

Busby worked mostly from odds and ends he saved during his career building houses and factories in the farming communities south of Birmingham.

He also painted on biscuit-shaped rocks, which he'd keep in his car to give to people he'd meet. Busby called them his "pet rocks."

"Wherever he traveled, far and wide, he'd take those rocks with him," Mrs. Hilyer says. "There are probably people all over Alabama who have his pet rocks."

In the early 1990s, not long after his wife moved into a nursing home, Busby had a heart attack. He, too, eventually settled into a nursing home. He died in 1992, just nine months after the death of his wife.

When she was cleaning out her parents' house after their deaths, Mrs. Hilyer came across photographs of some of the many strangers who had visited her father. "A lot of people would drop by and take pictures, and they'd usually send him copies," she says.

"He loved the company. Our family was the type that always liked a crowd. My dad was always happy. If he was worried or concerned about something, most of the time, you'd never know it."

Sarah, Junior, and Manuel Murphy, *ca. 1986.*
Mixed media on wood. Dimensions: 41", 39", 46" h.
Collection of Micki Beth Stiller.

CHRIS CLARK

Born October 25, 1958, in Birmingham, Alabama
Lives in Birmingham

When Chris Clark's grandmother first saw one of his painted quilts, she told him, "Now what do you want to go and do that for? That paint's just gonna come right off when you put it in the washer."

Clark explained that he intended the quilt be used as a wall hanging, not to add warmth and comfort to somebody's bed. But his grandmother just couldn't go along with it.

"Surprisingly enough, the first five or six people I showed the quilts to all thought the same thing, that no, you shouldn't be doing that, that's not the way it's done," Clark recalls.

"And it was really discouraging. People thought I was kind of crazy for doing it. But I kept making them. I just stopped showing them to anybody."

A large man with a soft-spoken, sweet demeanor, Clark has covered the walls of his small rented art studio in Birmingham, Alabama, with a dozen of his hand-painted quilts. They are among the 100 or so he's made since he showed his disapproving grandmother that first painted quilt in 1991.

One quilt on display in his studio is filled with panels depicting the stories of Noah and the Ark, the Sermon on the Mount, and other scenes from the Bible. Clark's favorite quilt, called "The Church," takes up nearly an entire wall and features a colorfully robed gospel choir serenading a swaying congregation.

Another quilt, "Play Time," shows children frolicking in a park, playing hopscotch, chasing balls and swinging high into the air.

"Most of my art, now, does have children in it," Clark says. "My first work was kind of sad. But when I started on 'Play Time,' I was real happy, thinking about the games I played as a child. I've been painting happier since then, I think."

As a boy growing up in west Birmingham, Clark never figured he'd end up an artist. Yet he did have the feeling he had something special to offer the world. "Somehow, I felt there was something I'd do one day to make me famous or known. But I wouldn't have said art."

Clark's parents divorced when he was young, and his mother, who worked in a laundry, raised her five children alone. Young Chris often visited his grandmother's Pratt City home—a long, tunnel-like dwelling, or "shotgun house," that would later show up in his art.

"You could open the front door and see all the way through the back door," he recalls. "You could ride a bike through there pretty easy."

Raised in the Baptist church, Clark attended local public schools and was graduated from Ensley High School in 1977. He enrolled in Livingston University with his sights set on becoming a teacher. But after three years of partying and not much studying, he dropped out and joined the army.

"I was bored with school. Instead of being there for an education, I was having fun. I thought I needed to get away from all that. And I wanted to see the world."

His new military life first took him to Kentucky and finally to Frankfurt, Germany, where he was stationed for the last four years of his seven-year hitch. There, he saw the world, or at least part of Europe. He also married and had a daughter, now eight years old.

In 1988, after his discharge from the service, Clark returned to Birmingham and took a job in a masonry factory.

24

Chris Clark   1/21/94   Birmingham, Alabama

When the factory closed, Clark found similar work, but again was laid off when that company went out of business.

During his last layoff in 1990, Clark began to feel ill, but he had no money or insurance to pay for a doctor. What disturbed him most was his increasingly blurry vision. "My eyesight would come and go, like the clouds out there," he says. "It would get real gray sometimes. I didn't know what was wrong with me, but I kind of thought I was dying."

It was then that he decided to start painting. "I'd always wanted to draw and paint, and all of a sudden it hit me that I better start, because I was going to lose my sight."

Clark's grandmother finally took him to a doctor, who diagnosed severe diabetes. Even as Clark improved under medical attention, his eyesight remained blurry for months, hindering his search for a job. "I'd go out in the morning to look for a job, and that's when my sight was the worst," Clark says.

"I'd try to fill out the job applications, but I couldn't see them too good. One time this guy caught me asking another person to read the application for me. He thought I couldn't read."

So during his long days at home, Clark—who had separated from his wife and was staying with his mother and grandmother—painted pictures, usually on slabs of wood he found at flea markets. He would draw and paint scenes of people fishing, washing clothes, or performing other rituals of daily life. While Clark painted, his grandmother, a quilter, was busy nearby with her thread and needle.

One day, Clark asked her to show him how to quilt. She taught him the basic stitches, passed down from her grandmother, and soon Clark had stitched together his own little quilt.

"My first instinct was to paint it," he says. "I hadn't set out to do that. But I painted a picture on it, and the picture was just beautiful. So I did another one."

Clark worried that the quilts were soaking up vast quantities of paint, so he began experimenting with ways to keep the acrylic paint on top of the fabric. He settled on a mixture of fabric dye and paint, coated with polyurethane.

While Clark's relatives didn't appreciate his painted quilts, he soon found an admirer at a local flea market, where he began selling his wood-block paintings. A woman asked if he also painted on canvas, and he said no, but then he told her about the quilts. When she saw them, she paid him $100 each for two painted quilts and encouraged him to continue the work.

Clark soon made friends in the art world, and by 1991, his painted quilts were selling for hundreds of dollars in folk art galleries in Birmingham and Montgomery.

Clark, who lives with his mother in the Birmingham neighborhood of Ensley, supplements his income by giving art lessons to schoolchildren. He never forgets the single dismal art course he took in college, and how his professor took one look at his folksy drawings and told him he wasn't cut out to be an artist. "He said, 'Don't even think about it,' " Clark recalls.

"I tell these kids that I don't care how they draw something, as long as they express what they're trying to say and get their emotions out. With my quilts, that's what I've always tried to do."

27

The Church, *1992.*
Acrylics, cotton, cotton blends, synthetics. Dimensions: 72" x 53".
Collection of Rena Selfe.

Five Loaves and Two Fishes, *1993.*
Acrylics, cotton, cotton blends. Dimensions: 67" x 47".
Birmingham Museum of Art, Birmingham, Alabama.
Gift of Rena Selfe.

WILLIAM DAWSON

Born October 20, 1901, near Huntsville, Alabama
Died June 1990, in Chicago, Illinois

William Dawson traveled to Washington, D.C., in 1982 for the opening of an important show, "Black Folk Art in America, 1930-1980," at the Corcoran Gallery of Art.

He was among the 20 self-taught artists whose work was featured in that landmark exhibition. And while Dawson said it was among the highlights of his life to be included, the fancy goings-on in the capital didn't intimidate him at all.

Susann Craig, who had befriended Dawson in Chicago years earlier and gave him his first solo art show (at Chicago's Columbia College), recalls how the artist made some powerful friends during that Washington visit.

"Nancy Reagan, early in the day, came and had a private showing at the gallery," Ms. Craig says. "And Mr. Dawson just went right up to her and just took her right around and showed her the exhibit. She loved it, I think. It was really a hoot."

Dawson could charm almost anybody with his outgoing personality and total confidence and pride in his work. "I remember taking him once to a group show where some of his things were included, and he just kept walking around shaking his head," Ms. Craig says. "He said his things were so much better than the others. He just couldn't understand it."

It was Ms. Craig, a Chicago resident and long-time folk art collector, who "discovered" Dawson 20 years ago, in the early days of his woodcarving hobby. She was visiting her neighborhood library when a display of art caught her attention.

"It was an exhibit of work by some local senior citizens, and Mr. Dawson's things were included. At that time, he was doing little horse-drawn carts. I thought they were so wonderful that I got his name and went and visited him."

Ms. Craig soon introduced Dawson to others, including Chicago artist Roger Brown and gallery owner Phyllis Kind, who would help bring his work to a larger audience.

By the time Ms. Craig met him, Dawson was already disenchanted with the art lessons he was taking at the senior citizens center. "He was pretty much deciding that he knew more than the people at the center and was going to go out on his own," she recalls.

Dawson lived with his wife, Osceola, in a two-bedroom Chicago apartment, where he spent the last two decades of his

Photo by Chuck Rosenak. Courtesy Museum of American Folk Art.

Tiger, *ca. 1980.*
Mixed media on paper. Dimensions: 9 1/2" x 15".
Robert Cargo Folk Art Gallery, Tuscaloosa, Alabama.

WILLIAM DAWSON

life carving figurines of animals and people. He worked most-ly with wood salvaged from broken furniture.

For his humorous "Female Figure With A Red Dress," Dawson used a pair of old bowling pins to create his wooden woman's curvaceous legs. Dawson was known, too, for his totem poles, carved from the discarded chair and table legs that he found during neighborhood forays in search of junk.

"I see something lying in the street and I know it could be turned into something," Dawson told writer Ruth Ann Stewart in 1990. "I don't know what I'm going to do when I pick up a piece of wood, but the longer I look at it, it comes to me."

For her essay accompanying the 1990 exhibition "The Artworks of William Dawson" at the Chicago Public Library Cultural Center, Ms. Stewart spoke with the artist about his long-ago life in Alabama.

Born near Huntsville, he grew up on a 665-acre farm owned by his grandfather. Dawson's father, Johnny, was a part-time farmer primarily interested in breeding horses. Although his mother, Lavenia, was protective of her young son, he was free to roam the farm on horseback with his brother Leroy.

His mother and grandfather had high hopes for young William Dawson, but his education didn't extend beyond grade school. He eventually headed to Chicago, where he found work as a bellboy. He returned to Alabama long enough to get married and have a daughter. In 1923, Dawson moved his family to Chicago. He went to work for a produce distributor in South Water Market, a bustling commercial district.

Dawson was such a good worker that by the time he retired in 1965, he was in charge of the company's shipping dock and had a number of other important duties. In retire-ment, he worked part-time as a security guard. It was during stretches of guard duty that he started carving small figurines out of old furniture wood.

Dawson eventually signed up for art lessons at a local senior citizens center, where he tried everything from clay work to painting. His favorite art form, however, remained wood-carving, and the small apartment he shared with Osceola began to fill up with his "toys," as he called his figurines.

His rural background inspired many of his carvings and paintings, which often depicted animals in bucolic surround-ings. He also was influenced by the images he saw on televi-sion. His "Chicken George" carving, depicting a man with a chicken perched on his head, was inspired by the television miniseries "Roots." Some of his carvings are of politicians and entertainers, such as Sammy Davis, Jr. and Tina Turner.

He colored most of his work with acrylic paint and added unexpected flourishes. "He once made a figure that was sup-posed to be Mayor (Richard J.) Daley," Susann Craig recalls. "He used a piece of his wife's hair to glue on top, and it didn't look anything like Mayor Daley."

To help make his carving easier, Dawson fashioned a lathe from the motor of his wife's sewing machine. "That's how he was shaping some of the totem poles," Ms. Craig says.

Soft-spoken and gentlemanly, Dawson delighted in the visitors who came to his home. And he took great pride in see-ing the shows and exhibitions of his work. He was especially pleased with the 1990 Chicago Cultural Center exhibit, which took place not long before his death.

Dawson was into his eighties when that exhibition was mounted, and he seemed to worry that his time was growing short. Yet his high opinion of his own talent never wavered. As he told Ms. Stewart, "If God will spare me and give me time to keep on, I'll be up there with Picasso."

30

Totem with Three Heads and One House, *ca. 1977.*
Paint and varnish on wood. Dimensions: 17 ½" h.
Collection of Susann Craig.

WILLIAM DAWSON

32

Bird, 1988.
Acrylic, enamel, and pencil on paper. Dimensions: 10" x 13 ¾".
Collection of Kurt Gitter and Alice Yelen.

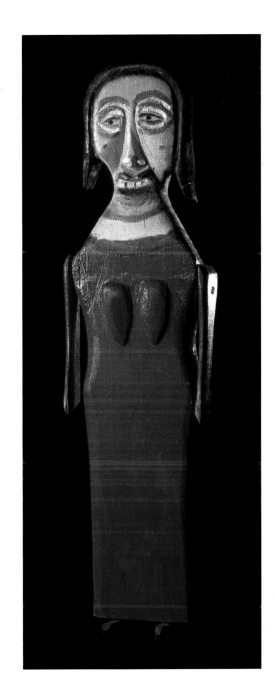

33

Woman, *1988.*
House paint on wood. Dimensions: 28" h.
Robert Cargo Folk Art Gallery, Tuscaloosa, Alabama.

THORNTON DIAL

On a cold autumn Saturday afternoon, Thornton Dial stands in a pasture among an assortment of goats and pigs, looking like a man who's found paradise.

A rooster crows, and Dial listens, then offers up an old wives' tale he swears he believes. "When somebody dies, them roosters'll take to crowin', " he says, his gold front tooth gleaming in the sun. "You might not believe it, but I know it's true."

Dial's pasture is nestled in rural west Jefferson County, Alabama, among 22 acres that include a sprawling house and a separate garage studio. There, the retired laborer turns the truth, as he knows it, into art that sells for thousands of dollars. A massive painting-in-progress called "Mercedes Benz Plant Coming To Alabama" incorporates an actual steering wheel, muffler, and other automotive parts. Dial started the piece after learning Mercedes is building a new plant in the nearby town of Vance. "I think it's great, and that's why I did this," Dial explains in his customary no-nonsense manner.

An older piece, called "The Jungle," features an almost life-size tiger, made from salvaged rubber, wandering across a canvas painted jungle green. "I just had me the idea to make a piece about the jungle and the struggling tiger," Dial says.

Wild animals, especially tigers, show up often in his work and represent, to the artist, both struggle and invincibility. "He be something like the king of the jungle, a symbol of people's life," Dial told *Birmingham* magazine writer Ruth Reuse a few years back.

On this cold afternoon, as he contemplates "The Jungle," Dial looks at the tiger and softly says, "There was a man at Pullman's, where I used to work, whose name was Tiger, and he used to struggle for the union. Everything in life is a struggle. That's what I'm trying to say here."

Struggle is something Dial knows well. For many years, he worked too hard and earned too little, carrying ice, cutting hay, fixing pipes, and laying bricks, always wondering if he'd have enough money to make ends meet. His most enduring career was as a helper at the Pullman Standard Company, a Bessemer, Alabama, boxcar manufacturing plant that closed in 1980.

"All my work has been hard," Dial says. "All my days, anything I ever did been hard and rough. That's the truth. That's what made me do the things I do. Because you want to have something, but you are not able to have it. I just wanted things of my own all my life."

Born in rural Sumter County, Alabama, to a young woman with no means to care for him, Dial spent his early years with his great-grandmother. He attended school sporadically, staying out many days to work in the fields picking corn and sweet potatoes.

"I didn't never have to go to school too much in my lifetime," says Dial, who finished the third grade and never went back. "I had to work a lot of the time. Sometimes, I was just shootin' hookey."

After his great-grandmother died when he was ten, Dial lived with an aunt for several years. At age 13, he moved to Bessemer to live with other relatives, his aunt Sarah Lockett and her husband, David, whom Dial came to look upon as his parents. To this day, he still makes daily visits to the home of Mrs. Lockett, now a widow well into her nineties.

By the time he moved in with the couple, Thornton was already adept at making things. He turned junked machine

Thornton Dial Sr.   10/30/93   McCalla, Alabama

parts into toys. Intensely curious, he entertained himself by taking things apart, including farm animals. "I used to cut up hogs, cut up frogs," he says. "I called myself operatin' on things."

Clara Dial, married to Thornton for four decades, knew him when both were youngsters in Bessemer. "He and my uncle used to like to stand on the corner and box," she recalls.

Throughout their marriage, and especially after his layoff from Pullman Standard, Dial made things with tin cans, cement, and spare parts, often to the embarrassment of Clara, who viewed the stuff as junk. "When he was making things, he had to turn on the gas to melt the plastic, and I used to fuss about him running up the gas bill," she says. "I thought he was wasting his time."

In the early 1980s, Dial and his sons formed a backyard business, making patio furniture from strips of steel. It wasn't until the mid-1980s, when Dial sold a piece of his "junk"—an iron turkey—to Atlanta art dealer and collector Bill Arnett for $200, that his wife and five children really began to recognize his unique talent. But first they had to get over the shock, as did Dial. "I felt like that man was crazy to give me that two hundred dollars for a turkey," Dial says. "I only asked for twenty-five dollars."

Another self-taught Alabama artist, Lonnie Holley, who had met Dial through a family friend, introduced him to Arnett. In the years since he bought that $200 turkey, Arnett has served as Dial's mentor, agent, and sole representative in the art world.

The partnership, according to Dial, has been satisfactory. It was Arnett, he says, who encouraged him to paint and to incorporate found objects into his paintings. One such piece, Dial says, sold for close to $100,000.

Anyone who knew Dial a decade ago knows just how far he's come, both in his art and his lifestyle. In the mid 1980s,

the Dials were living in a poor neighborhood in Bessemer. By 1990, Dial was successful enough as an artist to move to the sprawling house and accompanying acreage–complete with private lake and an assortment of beloved farm animals–he now calls home.

Dial traveled to New York City in late 1993 for the openings of a pair of one-man shows of his work–at the Museum of American Folk Art and the New Museum of Contemporary Art. "All that has come to be, I always saw in my life and my dreams," Dial says. "I always knew."

Dial's success has spawned the artistic careers of a number of his relatives, including his son Thornton Jr., his brother Arthur, and nephews Richard Dial and Ronald Lockett. For all of his acclaim, Dial remains quiet and unassuming and seems to prefer staying out of the spotlight. Once embarrassed about his lack of education, Dial (who never learned to read or write) has come to see his deficiency in perspective. "It's kind of like a blind man," he says of his illiteracy. "Everybody's blind in something."

That wisdom permeates his work, which often comments on social problems and world events. Dial offers his more complex art for sale. His home is decorated with his wife's private Thornton Dial collection of whimsical paintings, including a portrait of Stevie Wonder and a pair of charcoal and watercolor renderings of another favorite Dial subject, the female body.

Although Clara Dial has come to recognize and appreciate her husband's talent, she says he was a wonderful man before he had any money. "I'm proud of him, but when he makes me mad, I still fuss," she says. Dial, too, seems happy with his work and his reward. "I'm proud something good happened before I died," he declares.

The Tiger Will Climb, The Bird Will Fly, *1992.*
Charcoal and watercolor on paper. Dimensions: 30" x 22".
Luise Ross Gallery, New York, New York. Photograph courtesy Luise Ross Gallery.

38

Rolling Tiger, *1993.*
Mixed media on board. Dimensions: 52" x 52".
Luise Ross Gallery, New York, New York. Photograph courtesy Luise Ross Gallery.

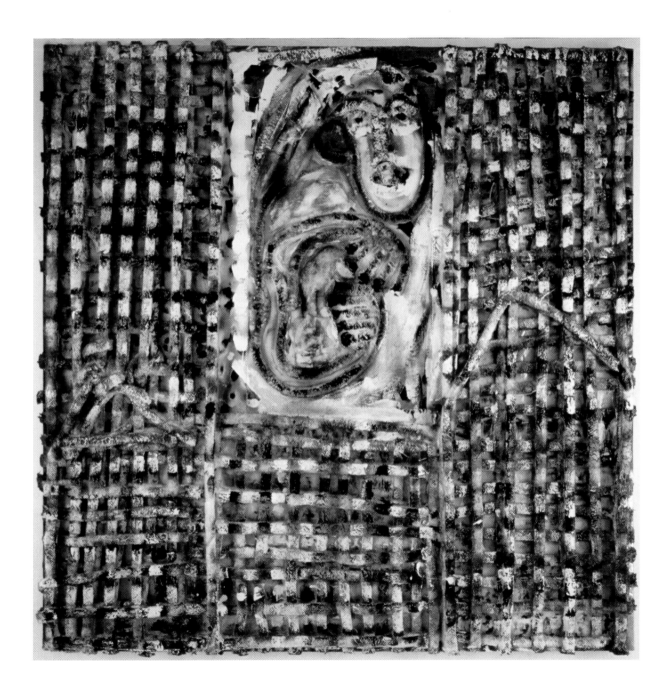

Jailhouse, *1993.*
Mixed media on canvas and wood. Dimensions: 48" x 48".
Luise Ross Gallery, New York, New York. Photograph courtesy Luise Ross Gallery.

40

A Blue Bird Will Make a Red Egg Hatch, *1993.*
Graphite, pastels, charcoal, ivory black pencil. Dimensions: 44" x 30".
Collection of William Arnett.

41

Wondering About Life in the Jungle, *1991.*
Watercolor on paper. Dimensions: 22" x 30".
Clary Sage Gallery, Birmingham, Alabama.

Easy Told: A Travelling Lie, *1993.*
Enamel, fabric, carpet, wire, plastic, metal, cardboard on canvas. Dimensions: 40 1/2" x 41".
Collection of William Arnett.

Little People Want to Play the Game, *1993.*
Enamel, spray paint, fabric, carpet, metal on canvas. Dimensions: 48" x 40".
Collection of William Arnett.

WILLIE LEROY ELLIOTT, JR.

**Born October 5, 1943, near Mobile, Alabama
Lives in Mobile**

For a quarter of a century, Willie Leroy Elliott, Jr. earned his living in Michigan's automotive industry. He worked in the machine shops and manufacturing plants around Detroit, where he performed numbingly repetitive duties that left him exhausted and unfulfilled at the end of the day.

It was good money, though, for a logger's son from Alabama. And with a wife and seven children, Elliott had no choice but to stay on in the plants and look for a creative outlet somewhere else.

He found it in his backyard, with a welding torch in his hand. He took junked car parts and turned them into metal sculptures that decorated his property and ignited an artistic drive he never suspected he had.

"I felt like I just wanted something to do," he says of the day in 1983 when he first started tinkering with the scrap metal he'd picked up in alleys near his house.

"When you're working industrial jobs, things like that, and you're sitting down, standing up, just packing parts all day long like I was, you get bored. When I went home, I didn't have much to do, other than play baseball or go bowling. In my spare time, I'd just be sitting around.

"So I went out and bought myself a welder. A fellow there at work showed me how to use it. I started tinkering around with some little pieces. From that, I advanced on to other things."

By the time Elliott moved back to Alabama in the summer of 1993, he had created about 250 metal and wood sculptures and seen his work featured in more than a dozen museum exhibitions and gallery shows. That last fact makes him especially proud. "I work hard and I try hard. I love doing it, and I guess that's what makes a difference."

Elliott's earliest sculptures resembled robots—little men in space-age getups adorned with all manner of metal gadgets. One of his favorite pieces was a variation on the robot—a waist-high metal man Elliott named "The Mechanic" because he was made entirely of wrenches.

As Elliott made more and more sculptures, he began to incorporate themes and offer his insights on social issues. He also began using a wider variety of salvaged items. For his piece called "Survival," he included stainless steel, bits of glass, and pieces of tail pipes. On one end of the artwork sits a happy cat; on the other, a bird.

"The message in 'Survival' is, you look at cats and birds and dogs, and they all seem to survive better than mankind. We are always killing each other. That was my message, that we need to take a clear look at our own selves, and then how the birds and the animals seem to get along, except when they're fussing over food or something. We have everything, and we're still trying to kill each other."

Using metal and wood, Elliott fashioned a number of furniture items, including chairs and settees. For his bench shaped like an elephant, he found a deer antler in the woods and used it to make the elephant's tusks.

Elliott's wife, Evelyn Lynn, wasn't impressed at first with his backyard sculptures. But in 1988, when he took a carload of his pieces to the Detroit Artists Market and sold them all in about 15 minutes, his wife quickly changed her opinion.

"All this is something like a new toy to me," Elliott says. "The more you play with it, the more excitement you get out of

Willie Leroy Elliott Jr.   12/17/93   Mobile, Alabama

it. There are so many ways you can do things, create things, especially welding things together. You take these images out of your mind. It's like I'm the computer, and my welder is my machine, and it just goes from there."

Elliott has never had an art lesson or, until 1983, any desire to create. "While I was in school, I don't think I ever picked up an art book, unless I was just flipping through the pages."

Born in the community of Franksville, just north of Mobile, Willie Leroy was the first of 11 children. His father was a logger and construction worker, and his mother stayed home to tend to the children.

Elliott went to schools in Franksville until he was 13, when his family moved to Mobile. He graduated from high school there in 1961. After attending trade school to study electric appliance repair and house wiring, he decided to head for Detroit and the booming automobile industry.

From 1965 until 1988, he held a variety of jobs in the factories and plants around the Motor City. He got married, had children and found time to study electrical engineering at an Ypsilanti community college.

In 1988, he accepted a buyout offer from General Motors, where he had worked full-time for a number of years. Wanting more time to devote to his art, Elliott figured he could find part-time work until he was old enough to draw his pension. But after toiling in a series of low-paying labor jobs and earning even less as a gardener, he decided the best thing to do was go home to Alabama.

He and Evelyn Lynn have settled into a rented house in Prichard, not far from where Elliott was born. He has a small studio behind the house, where he continues to create metal sculptures. He also has taken up painting on canvas, producing pictures of boys fishing and other scenes from his childhood.

His work is on sale in galleries in Chicago and New York, where the prices are as high as $4,800. Yet he doesn't sell enough to pay the rent. Evelyn Lynn works full-time in Mobile at a center for retarded people. And Elliott is still looking for part-time work.

He's determined to continue his art, even if it means doing without. "It's what I like doing, so I'll do anything I can to keep it coming," he says.

"It's like writing a song or something. If the urge hits me, and I want to go out here and do this, then nothin's gonna stop me. I'm going out there and get the parts I need, and my mind ain't gonna be happy 'til I make something."

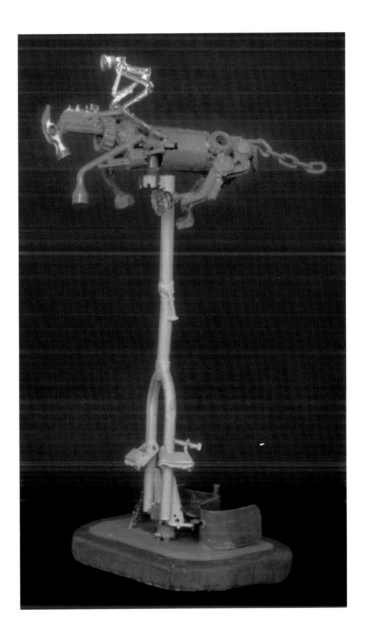

Tribute to Mary, *ca. 1990.*
Wood, metal, wire, paint. Dimensions: 54" h.
Artist's Collection.

Trade Zone, *1993.*
Car parts, metal, tools, found objects, paint. Dimensions: 42" h.
Artist's Collection.

NORA EZELL

Born June 24, 1919, in Brooksville, Mississippi
Lives in Tuscaloosa, Alabama

In the den of her tidy frame house, Nora Ezell has set up a card table next to her favorite chair. There, stretching her feet toward a portable heater, she sits for hours at a time, piecing together quilts with her crooked, arthritic fingers.

Although she often works with traditional patterns, including the popular wedding-ring design, Mrs. Ezell has made a name for herself in the last decade with her remarkable story quilts—that is, quilts whose panels not only are intricately hand-sewn but also tell a story.

In her quilt honoring Dr. Martin Luther King, Jr., Mrs. Ezell depicted important places and events in King's life, from the Dexter Avenue Baptist Church in Montgomery, Alabama, where he once preached, to the Edmund Pettus Bridge he marched across in nearby Selma during the 1960s' struggle for civil rights.

Another of her quilts, commissioned by the Birmingham Civil Rights Institute, is filled with pictures of the churches that helped define the movement. Among them is Birmingham's Sixteenth Street Baptist Church, where four black girls died in a Ku Klux Klan bombing in 1963.

The quilt, called "A Tribute to Civil Righters of Alabama," also contains the names of such civil rights figures as Autherine Lucy, the first black student to attend the University of Alabama, and Eugene "Bull" Connor, the infamous Birmingham police commissioner. Mrs. Ezell stitches the scenes freehand, as if she were painting a picture. She keeps a journal for each story quilt, logging the hours she spent making it and the amount of material it required. The King quilt alone took her 586 hours to complete. Some take as long as 1,500 hours.

"There's no way in the world anybody could pay me for a story quilt if I really charged what I ought to charge," Mrs. Ezell says. "This is hard work. And I don't work by no pattern. I just do what comes into my mind."

Some of her themes are serious and sad; others are funny and playful. Among her quilts-in-progress is a raised-work piece commemorating baseball's outstanding players. The panels feature cartoon-like portraits of Willie Mays, Johnny Bench, Hank Aaron, and others, decked out in their baseball splendor.

A recently finished three-dimensional quilt, "Children of the World," features children of a variety of cultures and nationalities.

Although she's been making story quilts for just a dozen years, Nora Ezell has received national recognition. Two of her quilts were included in a major exhibition, "Stitching Memories African-American Story Quilts." That show, put together by the Williams College Museum of Art in Williamstown, Massachusetts, toured the country from 1989 to 1991.

In 1990, the Alabama State Council on the Arts bestowed on her its Alabama Folk Heritage Award. In 1992, the National Endowment for the Arts named her a Master Traditional Artist and awarded her a National Heritage Fellowship.

A delighted Nora Ezell, accompanied by her grandson David, flew to Washington, D.C., to receive the NEA award, which carried with it a $5,000 prize. Before she cashed the check, she made a copy and inserted it into her scrapbook, next to newspaper clippings about her achievement.

"I got to meet George Bush," Mrs. Ezell says. "He was in a hurry that day, and he just kind of reached out and started shaking people's hands. I reached over and just kind of touched him. I said I'd never wash that hand, but I did."

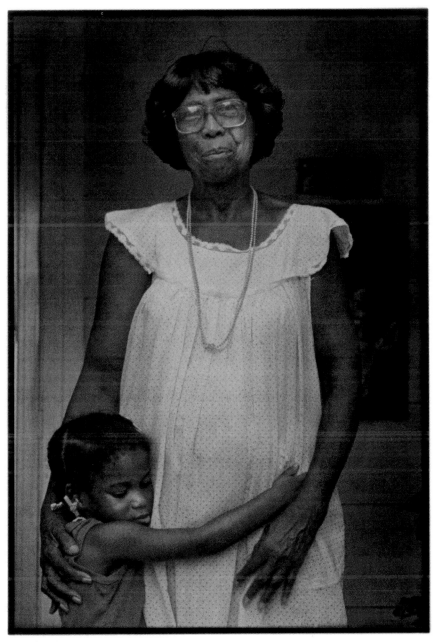

Nora Ezell   8/15/93   Tuscaloosa, Alabama

Sitting in her living room with the scrapbook in her lap, Mrs. Ezell turns the pages, pausing to recall the highlights of the Washington trip. "I wore a beautiful dress to the Heritage Awards banquet. My grandson told me I looked so pretty, and I felt young and good. I said grace at our table that night, and it was something to remember."

A page in the scrapbook reminds her of something funny, and she throws her head back and laughs. "A bus driver up in Washington told us we were too intelligent to stay in Alabama," she says.

Although she dropped out of school in the eleventh grade, Nora Ezell prides herself on her intelligence, and she is knowledgeable on a variety of subjects. She admires simplicity but has no tolerance for stupidity or shoddy work. For that reason, she's learned to perform a variety of tasks most people would hire somebody else to do.

When she moved from rural Greene County, Alabama, to Tuscaloosa a year or so ago, she alone did the renovations on her new house. She painted, installed new carpet, hung wallpaper, made new curtains, and even delivered and arranged her furniture, one pickup truckload at a time.

"I'd just as soon do it myself and get a poor job than to pay somebody and get a poor job," she says. "I can't afford to pay somebody anyway."

Born in Brooksville, Mississippi, into a family of ten children, young Nora used to watch her mother make quilts and sew clothes for the family. "She didn't teach me to quilt. I would fan her with cardboard while she was working, so naturally I'd watch what she was doing. But I taught myself."

Her father, a farmer, moved the family to Fairfield, Alabama, when Nora was about four years old. There, he went to work for the old Tennessee Coal and Iron Company. Nora

and her eight sisters and one brother attended the company-run schools, where she took her first and only sewing lesson.

At home, she and her sisters sewed their own clothes under the watchful eye of their mother, who insisted things be done right. Nora soon adopted her mother's perfectionism, which served her well in school. She excelled in math and science.

In the eleventh grade, she quit school to get married, thinking she would return and complete her education. But then her daughter, Annie Ruth, was born, and her husband ran off to New York. Nora had no choice but to go to work. She and Annie Ruth moved in with a relative in Pickens County, Alabama. There, Nora picked cotton and worked as a maid.

Years later, after her daughter was grown and her husband had died, Nora married again and moved with her new husband, Joseph Ezell, to Paterson, New Jersey. He took a job with the city, and she went to work in the garment factories, learning all she could about fabric and the craft of sewing.

She also waged a battle against cancer in 1970, undergoing a radical mastectomy and radiation therapy. She seemingly beat the disease, but Annie Ruth wasn't so lucky. It was Annie Ruth's diagnosis of cancer in the early 1980s that led to her mother's renewed interest in quilting.

To cheer her daughter during the difficult days of treatment, Nora—who had moved back to Alabama with her husband in the late 1970s—took Annie Ruth on a series of outings. During one such trip, they went to an area arts and crafts fair, where the quilts caught their attention. One quilt, honoring the University of Alabama, contained "nothin' but Bear Bryant's hat and a bunch of footballs," as Mrs. Ezell tells it.

She and Annie Ruth were not impressed. On the drive home, Nora resolved to make a better University of Alabama quilt. With ideas from Annie Ruth and her grandchildren, she

Music is the Universal Language, *1992.*
Cotton, synthetics, knitted yarn. Dimensions: 75" x 84".
Birmingham Jazz Hall of Fame. Gift of Roberta Lowe.

crafted a quilt that featured not only Bear Bryant's hat and a football but also the famous Denny Chimes bell tower, a baseball and basketball, schoolbooks, and even the schoolhouse doors once blocked by Governor George Wallace.

The quilt inspired both Nora and her daughter, who was growing increasingly ill. Their next project, the Martin Luther King, Jr., quilt, was half finished in 1984 when Annie Ruth died.

Mrs. Ezell was so distraught that she didn't work on the quilt for another two years. When it was finally finished, she displayed it at a Tuscaloosa crafts fair, where she and her quilt drew a lot of attention. Soon she was getting calls from the state arts council people, who encouraged her with words and money to continue her work.

And so she has. Quilting has kept her busy in the lonely days without her daughter and, more recently, her husband, who died in 1986. She has enjoyed the attention her work has received, but she takes exception to the folklife scholars who have labeled her an African-American quilter.

"Everybody calls me that, and I resent it. I'm just as much an American as anybody else. So don't call me an African-American nothin'. I ain't got no heritage in Africa. It's right here in the United States."

Tribute to Civil Righters in Alabama, *1989.*
Applique, cotton, embroidery, synthetics. Dimensions: 106" x 79".
Birmingham Civil Rights Institute.

REVEREND HOWARD FINSTER

**Born December 2, 1916, in Valley Head, Alabama
Lives in Summerville, Georgia**

hen I was born, seems like I remember somebody pickin' me up by the heels and me cryin', " says Howard Finster, sitting in his Paradise Garden art gallery on a chilly Sunday afternoon.

A small crowd has gathered around the famous preacher and artist, who is telling his life story for the third time in less than an hour. The visitors, their arms full of Finster's painted wooden cutout portraits of Elvis and Hank Williams and Henry Ford and Finster himself, listen politely and try to get in a question or two.

But a chat with Finster mostly involves your listening and his talking, and he's more prolific at talking than he is at painting. Like his art, his conversation is unpredictable and occasionally indecipherable, but never less than entertaining.

"Spider Man sat at my table at this Hollywood dinner," he tells a woman who has approached him for an autograph. A few minutes later, he's announcing to another stranger, "I never been arrested, never had a speeding ticket, never been drunk."

The visitors come and go, but Finster keeps talking–about himself, his art, and his views on religion. "I believe when you die you go to the First Heaven, where you meet Moses and your mother and everybody you know, and then you go to the Second Heaven, and there you don't remember nothin' about this world."

The visitors, always polite, nod as if they understand. They snap his picture and get his autograph and sometimes ask for special favors, as one betrothed couple does on this autumn Sunday. Just before 4 o'clock, the young man and woman, relatives in tow, arrive to be married by the Reverend Howard Finster at his famous homemade park known as Paradise Garden.

Finster clearly doesn't know the couple, but he's up for the ceremony. At 4 o'clock exactly, he's standing outdoors, near his towering World's Folk Art Church, with a Bible in his hand. The bride shivers in her flimsy white wedding gown. The grinning groom wears a black tuxedo and a diamond earring. Among their guests are men in suits and women in mink coats.

Wearing baggy green trousers, a green knitted cap, and an old brown coat with paint-stained cuffs, Finster combs his hair and addresses the gathering. "We're glad to see y'all here. This is one of the greatest events of life, intended to last for all time."

He begins the ceremony, pausing to offer anecdotes on his own marriage of more than 50 years. Finally, Finster pronounces the couple husband and wife. "Nobody's supposed to mess with y'all now, not your mama and daddy, nobody," he declares. "You've got a home of your own."

Finster's home, he likes to tell visitors, is "not of this world." Those who have met him, seen his art, heard his sermons, and listened to him describe his visions would probably agree that Finster is not your run-of-the-mill evangelical preacher.

Since bursting onto the folk art scene in the late 1970s with his distinct, other-worldly paintings, he has become the genre's superstar, written up in *The New York Times, The Washington Post, Life*, and even *Penthouse* magazine.

During a 1982 appearance on "The Tonight Show With Johnny Carson," Finster played his banjo and informed viewers that the world's two "beauty spots" could be found in Hollywood, California, and Summerville, Georgia, where he has lived since the 1960s.

Finster's paintings have adorned three album covers for the Athens, Georgia-based rock band R.E.M., and he counts the

Howard Finster   11/3/93   Summerville, Georgia

group members among his good friends. Another rock band, Talking Heads, paid him $4,200 to paint the jacket for the platinum-selling "Little Creatures" album, named by *Rolling Stone* magazine as the best album cover of 1985.

His paintings–typically scenes of a peculiar heaven, complete with angels flying around odd, wedding cake-shaped buildings–hang in galleries and museums around the world, including the Smithsonian Institution, which Finster calls the "Smithstonian" Institution.

For all the acclaim, Finster has remained true to his calling. And that, he says, is to spread the message of Jesus Christ. "People criticize me for associating with rock 'n' roll, but I reached more people with that one album cover than I reached in 45 years of preachin', " he said in a 1986 interview with the *Birmingham Post-Herald.* "I'm here for everybody. The infidels are my friends. I don't condemn 'em. You can't win people by condemnin' ."

And with that philosophy, he welcomes anybody and everybody to his Paradise Garden, two acres of once-swampy land that Finster has turned into an incredible maze of found-object sculpture and environmental art.

Located behind Finster's former residence in the community of Pennville, on the outskirts of Summerville, Georgia, the garden includes a winding concrete walkway embedded with marbles and bits of broken tile, mirrors, and colored glass. Lining the vine-covered walkway, which leads past Finster's cement sculptures and his tower of rusted bicycle parts, are junked tools, cars, machine parts, kitchen appliances, televisions, typewriters, and furniture. The collection of junk, Finster says, represents "the inventions of mankind."

Scattered about are a number of buildings of various shapes and sizes, all built by Finster from some divinely inspired blueprint in his mind. There's a tiny house made from

Coca Cola bottles; a long, raised, indoor gallery, where Finster displays other artists' work, along with news clippings about himself, and various gifts he's accumulated through the years; and, most spectacularly, the five-story, 16-sided, columned structure he calls the World's Folk Art Church.

Finster's plywood paintings are displayed throughout, along with signs containing Bible verses and warnings of the judgment day to come. There is also this prominent painted message, which looks like just another work of art and even bears Finster's autograph: "Not responsible for accidents. Howard Finster."

For years, Finster and his wife, Pauline, lived in one of the small bungalows at the front of Paradise Garden. The smaller house next door, which now serves as his art gallery, was where Finster spent most of his time, greeting guests and interviewers and often painting well into the night. Finster had an agreement with his wife: He could do whatever decorating he wanted in the garden and at his studio bungalow, as long as he didn't mess up the main house.

Several years ago, after Finster's art had brought him fame and fortune, the couple moved across Summerville into a sprawling, sparkling white home with a swimming pool. The only bit of yard art probably reflects Pauline's taste more than her husband's–a herd of plastic deer, grazing serenely on the front lawn. Finster now creates most of his art in a studio behind his new home, where he seems to concentrate on making the inexpensive wooden cutouts he sells at Paradise Garden. Also on sale there is art by his son, Roy, and grandson, Michael, plus a variety of Finster-related souvenirs, including Paradise Garden coffee mugs and tee-shirts.

The paintings that made Finster famous–depicting the mansions of heaven and his spectacular visions–now sell for thousands of dollars, well beyond the means of most of his guests.

Clock Case, *1976.*
Tractor enamel on wood. Dimensions: 11" h.
The Denton Collection.

REVEREND HOWARD FINSTER

The artist himself, who in the mid-1980s said he needed only three hours of sleep each night, admits he's slowed down considerably in recent years. "I'm gettin' bad about hearin' and seein' and havin' a steady hand," he says.

Yet his memory seems sharp as he tells folks of his humble upbringing just a short drive west of Summerville, in Valley Head, Alabama. His daddy was a sawmill lumberjack, and his mother worked the farm and took care of 13 children.

It was there, when Finster was three years old, that he had his first vision. He remembers it in detail. He says he was looking for his mother in a tomato patch when his dead sister appeared, wearing a white robe and walking down from heaven. Finster believes the vision was a message from God that he would one day be a visionary artist.

Later, with just a sixth-grade education, a teenage Howard Finster began preaching the gospel in country churches throughout Alabama, Georgia, and Tennessee. He spent weekdays working in factories and mills and, later, doing carpentry work, building clocks and repairing lawn mowers and bicycles.

He married Pauline Freeman in the 1930s, and by the early 1940s they had settled in Trion, Georgia. There, Finster built an early version of his Paradise Garden, complete with several buildings and vast displays of junk. But there wasn't enough space for what Finster had in mind. So in 1961, he moved his family to the property in Pennville, where he set about creating his incredible park.

It wasn't until the mid-1970s, when Finster had another vision, that he turned into what he considered an artist. Finishing a bike repair job, he used his finger to dab paint on the metal. When he looked at his fingertip, he saw a human face—a sign from God that he should paint sacred art, he says.

His first painting was a portrait of George Washington copied off a dirty dollar bill. Fueled by coffee and chewing tobacco, Finster was soon working almost around the clock, painting the intricate, futuristic scenes he saw in his dreams.

"I've had visions of things several years before they happened, and I do a little painting on 'em," he says. He tells a visitor that he dreamed about lasers and rocket missiles long before they were a reality. "When your visions come true, that gets you the publicity. I been on the front of *The Wall Street Journal.*"

As the new bride and groom and their small wedding party mill about in Finster's gallery, the artist poses for pictures and signs more autographs. And then he starts to tell, yet again, the fantastic story of Howard Finster, man of visions.

Alford Shorter, *1977.*
Linseed oil and tractor enamel on cardboard. Dimensions: 8" x 8".
The Denton Collection.

60

Noah's Ark, ca. 1977.
Tractor enamel on particle board. Dimensions: 18" x 36½".
Collection of Kurt Gitter and Alice Yelen.

The Hurricane House, #6617, *1987.*
Tractor enamel on masonite. Dimensions: 23" x 47 1/2".
The Denton Collection

62

My 5000th Piece, #5000, *1985.*
Tractor enamel on wood, antique frame. Dimensions: 18" x 16".
The Denton Collection.

Jesus Coming in the Clouds, #6653, *1987.*
Woodburned cutout on Plexiglas mirror, beads, tractor enamel on plywood.
Dimensions: 43" x 19 1/2". The Denton Collection.

SYBIL GIBSON

**Born February 18, 1908, in Dora, Alabama
Lives in Dunedin, Florida**

I n a nursing home room not much bigger than a closet, a woman with white hair and stooped shoulders uses her bed as a makeshift easel. She spreads a paint-splattered sheet of plastic across the covers and then reaches under the bed for a page of old newspaper to use as a canvas. Trays holding brushes and little jars of paint, mostly acrylic and watercolor, are behind her as she stands on the beige tile floor, hovering over her work.

"Until I do it, I don't know what it's going to be," explains Sybil Gibson as she looks down at her latest watercolor painting, which is beginning to resemble a landscape.

"I just go from one brush stroke to another, and I do it fast. Most of the time goes in waiting 'til the paint gets dry. But when I do it, I do it quick and fast. As soon as the idea comes, I use it real quick."

When she moved into the nursing home in 1991, Sybil hadn't held a paintbrush in four years. Cataracts and chronic diabetes had left her sick and blind. She believed she would never paint again. She was spending her days in darkness in a Jasper, Alabama, assisted-living residence when her daughter, Theresa Buchanan of Palm Harbor, Florida, arranged for her to undergo cataract surgery.

"It was like a miracle," Sybil says of the surgery. "When they took the bandages off, I could see. I never was able to see so well as I did then."

As soon as she moved from the hospital to the nursing home, not far from her daughter's home, Sybil began painting again. Her daughter, who agreed to serve as her agent, bought her paints and drawing paper. But Sybil preferred to work the way she always had—on newspaper, brown bags, and scraps of cardboard.

Although most of her recent paintings are simple depictions of women's faces, she also turns out florals and abstracts and prides herself on her continuing status as an experimentalist. "I'm a person who appreciates any artistic expression in any direction," she says. "So much of my work is just doing it to see what happens."

Dressed in a yellow and brown muumuu, tan bedroom slippers, and a white knitted shawl, Sybil seems sweet and grandmotherly, not at all like the eccentric and mysterious woman the newspapers used to report on years ago.

"There was a lot that was written that I know wasn't true, but I was so happy to have the attention that I never objected to it," she says.

Yet when she sits down and begins to reminisce, it becomes clear that Sybil Gibson is an unusual woman who has indeed led a curious life.

Her well-to-do father, Monroe Aaron, was a coal mine operator and banker in Walker County, Alabama. Her mother, Nora Reed Aaron, gave birth to eight children, though only six would live to be adults.

When Sybil was a child, the family moved from Dora to Cordova, where Monroe Aaron managed one of the mines. There, young Sybil went on solitary journeys to the nearby creek, where she pulled pebbles out of the water and used them to draw pictures of animals in the dirt or on large flat rocks.

"I loved that, getting these different colored pebbles and finding a big flat rock and drawing on it," she says.

She attended local public schools and, later, a private boarding school in Athens, Alabama. As soon as she got her high school diploma she married her high school sweetheart, Hugh Gibson, who worked as a bill collector in Jasper. Before

Sybil Gibson   10/23/93   Dunedin, Florida

the birth of their only child, Theresa, Sybil often accompanied him on his rounds.

The marriage, though, began to sour, and the baby did not solve the Gibsons' growing domestic problems. Sybil's father, upset about her marriage, convinced her she had made a mistake to wed Hugh Gibson and that she needed to return to school. After six years of marriage, Sybil divorced Gibson, left her daughter with her parents, and set off for college.

She attended a half dozen colleges in Alabama, taking a peculiar array of courses that included aeronautical engineering. "I liked to get the many viewpoints of the different instructors," she says.

She also took a single unfulfilling art course. "When I turned in my artwork, the teacher said it was too advanced for the class. I thought that meant I'd get an A for sure, but I got a D. She didn't believe that I had done it."

Mrs. Gibson earned a bachelor of science degree from Jacksonville State Teachers College (now Jacksonville State University). She taught school in Walker County until the late 1940s, when she decided to move to Florida.

"I had sinus trouble real bad, and I wanted to go to a better climate for my sinus trouble," she explains. "I got the geography book and looked where the frost belt was. I wanted to go somewhere warm."

She settled in Fort Myers and took a teaching job in nearby Bonita Springs. She eventually migrated to Miami, where, about 1950, she married David DeYarmon and took a job teaching fourth grade in Hialeah, Florida. (Although Sybil DeYarmon is still her legal name, she has continued to use the name Sybil Gibson in her art career.)

"The way I taught, I was an experimentalist," she recalls of those early days as a schoolteacher. "I would make assignments to the children, or maybe I'd tell a story, and I'd ask them to draw something that would highlight what I'd been telling them. I learned a lot from the children. They were learning, and I was learning."

After her second husband's death in 1958, Mrs. Gibson decided to take time off from teaching "just to do things I wanted to do." One late fall day in the early 1960s, while browsing in a department store in downtown Miami, she saw something that would change her life.

"This store had put out the Christmas paper, the gift wrap, and I was just spellbound by one design that I saw. I stood there and drank it in, and I said to myself, 'It's so beautiful, so charming, and yet so simple I could do it myself.' Then is when I got the light. I boarded a bus and went home and started painting. I painted sixteen pictures that afternoon.

"I stepped back, and they were impressionistic. I was, in my mind, judging from the impressionist paintings I had seen. But that wasn't what I was painting. I was painting my childhood memories. That's still the best way to start painting, because you're not copying. Your childhood memories are so different from anything else."

At first she painted animals and flowers. Then, inspired by recollections of the children she had taught, she painted scenes of little girls dancing or holding flowers. Although she had kept a good supply of brushes and paint from her days as a teacher, she didn't bother buying any canvas or paper.

"I remember when I located my paints, I wondered what I would paint on. I'd been saving grocery bags, and so the sixteen paintings I did were on sixteen big grocery bags. I just put the bags in a sink of water and they came apart at the seams. I smoothed them out on a porcelain-topped table I had. While they were still wet, I painted the pictures with the tempera, which was what I had used in the classroom with the children."

67

Untitled, *ca. 1975.*
Tempera on paper bag. Dimensions: 31" x 45". Gift to Fayette Art Museum, Fayette, Alabama,
from Mrs. Rex A. Brown, in memory of J. Spencer Black.

Painting on damp brown bags gave her work a dreamlike quality. Some of the pastel images seemed to be disappearing, ghostlike, into the heavy brown paper. Pleased with her work, Mrs. Gibson carried it to local galleries and museums, where she made friends and also sales. The first painting she sold brought her $6 and plenty of satisfaction. "I thought six dollars was pretty good for a used grocery bag."

During the next three decades, she immersed herself in her painting, often to the point of neglecting her household bills and other business. Although her earnings from art were small and sporadic, she had done well in an earlier hobby–playing the stock market. And until her father died in the 1950s, he made sure she had money for food and even bought her a duplex in Miami.

But by the late 1960s, Sybil was so wrapped up in the act of painting that she grew out of touch with family and friends, began mismanaging her money, and forgot to pay her bills.

In 1971, when the Miami Museum of Modern Art gave her a one-woman show, Sybil Gibson did not attend. Nobody–including the folks at the museum–seemed to know her whereabouts. A favorable review in *The Miami Herald* carried the headline, "Sybil Gibson, Artist, Where Are You?"

The newspaper reviewer, Griffin Smith, wrote, "I believe that I can say unequivocally that I have seldom seen more beautiful passages of painting than some of those to be found in the dream gardens and dream children that Sybil Gibson has put down on commonplace grocery sacks."

A month later, Howell Raines, a reporter with *The Birmingham News* (now an editor with *The New York Times*)

discovered Mrs. Gibson in Birmingham, where she had been living in seedy hotels, supported by a small pension and the occasional sale of her paintings.

Today, Sybil Gibson dismisses those reports of her disappearance and subsequent wanderings. "I knew where I was, so I couldn't have been missing," she says. She recalls that she left Miami about 1969 because she got homesick for her native Alabama, especially its plants.

"I had got to going on field trips in Miami, studying the flora, the plants and weeds and all that. And I got to thinking about the weeds that I grew up with, that I was most familiar with, and I got homesick to go back and see those weeds."

She says she returned to Alabama and got deep into the study of weeds–picking samples that she would carry to the library for identification. "They were giving me a show in Miami, and I was off studying the weeds. That's what I was doing, going on long field trips to vacant lots. That's where I was when they wrote all that."

Through the 1970s and much of the 1980s, Sybil was back and forth between Florida and Jasper, living occasionally with tolerant relatives, selling some artwork and making do with her meager income. That she was obsessed with her art was no surprise to her daughter, who had watched her become similarly obsessed with anything that interested her, from religion to the stock market to weeds.

"Painting is my happiness," Sybil Gibson says, shuffling down a hallway in the nursing home, gripping an aluminum walker splattered with paint. Her eyes are closed, and a sweet smile stretches across her face.

Untitled, *ca. 1975.*
Tempera on paper bag. Dimensions: 19½" x 13".
Collection of Jack and Margaret Black.

SYBIL GIBSON

Untitled, *ca. 1965.*
Acrylic and tempera on newspaper. Dimensions: 14½" x 23".
Collection of Theresa and Fred Buchanan.

Sybil's Early Manner of Painting, *ca. 1980.*
Tempera on paper bag. Dimensions: 37" x 20".
Robert Cargo Folk Art Gallery, Tuscaloosa, Alabama.

72

Untitled, *1977*.
Tempera on paper bag. Dimensions: 23 1/2" x 18 1/2".
Collection of Jack and Margaret Black.

Untitled, *ca. 1980.*
Tempera on cardboard. Dimensions: 24" x 18".
Robert Cargo Folk Art Gallery, Tuscaloosa, Alabama.

JOSEPH HARDIN

Born April 19, 1921, near Bessemer, Alabama
Died Christmas Day 1989, in Birmingham

Joe Hardin wanted to travel the world, but the closest he got was watching the Discovery Channel on cable TV. It was there, in that electronic box, that he saw the exotic images of animals and plants that populated so many of his paintings.

For most of his 68 years, Hardin was confined to a wheelchair. He had rheumatoid arthritis so crippling he was embarrassed to eat in public. Yet he managed to create haunting pictures of such intensity that they seemed to leap off the cardboard scraps they were painted on.

"I started [painting] in the seventies," Hardin told *Birmingham Post-Herald* reporter Elaine Witt in 1989, just months before his death. "I lived in a complex where all my neighbors were students. I had to do something because I was by myself all the time."

His earliest effort at art was to copy *Playboy* comic strips onto thin sheets of paper, hung in his apartment. The drawings delighted his neighbors and family, especially his sister, Marvin White, who suggested he paper his walls with his art.

Encouraged, Hardin began coloring his drawings with acrylic paints and ink. Besides plants and animals, his favorite subjects were female nudes, in part, he claimed, because women liked to buy such paintings.

Born near Bessemer, Alabama, Hardin grew up mostly in the Birmingham neighborhood of Fountain Heights, the second in a family of four children. His father was a railroad machinist, his mother a homemaker, and none of the family, according to his sister, showed any sign of artistic talent.

Hardin was a normal, healthy little boy who made excellent grades at Martin School. When he was about ten years old, though, he came down with a fever so severe, his sister recalls, that "you'd get near his bed and just feel the heat."

After a series of lengthy stays in the hospital, Hardin was diagnosed at age 13 with rheumatoid arthritis. On crutches, he went back to school, making excellent marks. But then, as Mrs. White recalls, "One morning Joe woke up and he couldn't move his legs, and it was like that from then on."

Because public schools at the time weren't equipped for wheelchairs, Hardin had to give up his formal education at age 14. He began spending long days at his parents' home, where

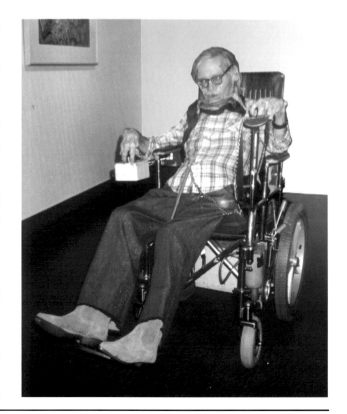

Photo courtesy Virginia Martin.

74

Untitled, *ca. 1987.*
Acrylic on mat board. Dimensions: 14" x 21½".
Micki Beth Stiller / Cottonbelt Gallery, Montgomery, Alabama.

he passed the time reading astronomy books and, in his first artistic endeavor, molding ashtrays and animals out of clay.

By 1945, both of Hardin's parents had died, and he was forced to move in with his sister, Marvin White, and her family. As Mrs. White recalls, "Joe just sat around a lot and didn't do much of anything. He didn't seem to know what he wanted to do, really, other than just read."

In an effort to be more independent, Hardin eventually moved into a nursing home. He quickly found it wasn't to his liking and moved back in with the Whites. After several more unsuccessful attempts at nursing-home living and a few lengthy visits with other relatives, Hardin decided that maybe he could do what an acquaintance with cerebral palsy had done—move into his own apartment.

So in the 1970s, Hardin rented a first-floor apartment on Birmingham's Southside, a haven for bohemian types of all persuasions. He wore his hair long and enjoyed sitting in front of his apartment, watching the parade of exotic humanity.

"I'd love to sit by the water fountain and watch the weirdos pass by," he said in the newspaper interview. "Well-dressed people, hippies, drunks. And the only ones that really speak to me are the hippies and drunks."

It was in that apartment that Hardin began drawing and painting. "Over there, I think he felt like he could do whatever he wanted, and it didn't matter whether he was messy or not," his sister says. "He felt like he wouldn't bother anybody."

"He'd probably been wanting to do those things for years and was just sitting around," she adds. "I wish he'd told somebody."

Marvin White's husband, James, took Hardin to buy art supplies, as did Hardin's growing number of friends attracted by his paintings. While Hardin's champions in the local art scene compared his work to that of Picasso and Matisse, his family viewed it primarily as therapy for Hardin. For the most part, they failed to appreciate it as art.

"I don't understand that kind of art," Mrs. White admits. "I mean, it's just, strange. It's gothic. I guess you have to know a lot about art to understand it. He must have been angry somewhere. Because it looks like anger to me."

His sister asked Hardin to paint pretty pictures of flowers. He told her he thought flowers were silly. "He did whatever came out of his mind, and some of 'em were weird to me," Mrs. White says.

During a chat with a visitor in her Birmingham home, Mrs. White rises from a blue velveteen chair and disappears down a hallway, returning moments later with two of her brother's pictures. One, an image of a horselike creature with a woman's breasts, appears to have been colored with green, yellow, red, and black crayons. "I can't make head nor tails of it," she says.

When she asked her brother to explain his artwork, Hardin would tell her, "You'll have to use your imagination."

If Hardin's family didn't understand his unique abilities, many trained artists did. Among them was Birmingham watercolor artist Virginia Martin, who heard about Hardin from a Meals-On-Wheels volunteer. Mrs. Martin introduced him to other artists and got him to join the Birmingham Art Association, which in 1987 displayed Hardin's work in a two-artist exhibit at the Birmingham Museum of Art. Other shows soon followed.

By then, Hardin—after being robbed at his Southside apartment—had moved to an apartment in North Birmingham. He wasn't fond of the neighborhood nor of the apartment building, which lacked handicapped-accessible plumbing. Friends and family did his grocery shopping while Hardin stayed busy painting.

Self-portrait, *1989.*
Mixed media on mat board. Dimensions: 16" x 12".
Robert Cargo Folk Art Gallery, Tuscaloosa, Alabama.

Months before he was discovered dead in his bed on Christmas Day 1989, Hardin had all but given up his art. He was in much pain and could hardly hold a paintbrush. "His hands looked like claws the last year or so," his sister says.

Yet his newfound status as an artist of merit, at least in Birmingham art circles, delighted him and kept him going, even as his health continued to fail.

Hardin never married, but he once came close. During one of his stays in a nursing home, he met a woman who also had severe arthritis, and the two wanted to wed. "Her daddy wouldn't let them," Mrs. White recalls. "He couldn't keep 'em both up. We said we'd help too, but he said no."

Dishwater blond, with blue eyes under horn-rimmed glasses, Hardin smoked generic cigarettes, which probably were responsible for his gruff speaking voice. He yearned to travel, to visit the places he'd read about or seen on TV. He talked often, too, of his keen desire to operate a ham radio, which would have allowed him to tour the world from his tiny apartment.

At his death, Hardin left little money and only a few paintings. Although late in his career he had earned as much as $100 each for his paintings, Hardin gave most of his art away or sold it for a few dollars.

Hardin, his sister suspects, would rather have been a scientist than an artist, but he seemed content with the way his life turned out.

"He had his happy moments," Mrs. White says. "He liked being around people. And he liked being written about in the paper. It made him feel great. He said it sort of makes up for a lot of things."

Untitled, *ca. 1987.*
Mixed media, artist's hair on mat board. Dimensions: 17 3/4" x 11 3/4".
Private Collection.

DAVID CHESLEY HARRIS

Born November 29, 1954, in Tulsa, Oklahoma
Lives in Mobile, Alabama

David Chesley Harris doesn't see much humor in the comedy of errors that has been his life for the past fifteen years.

He recounts each bit of bad luck with a deadpan delivery. There was the motorcycle wreck in 1979. Then the horseback riding accident a few months later. In 1980, during a vacation trip to Hawaii, his luggage disappeared and he ended up stranded, walking the streets by day, sleeping in shelters for the homeless at night.

Broke and hungry in Honolulu, he climbed high into a star fruit tree in search of lunch one day and tumbled backward to the ground, crushing eight bones in his left hand.

Although his recovery was long and painful, that accident was, in an ironic sense, Harris's lucky break. Amidst all his suffering, an artist was born. It happened one day during his recuperation. As he was strolling in downtown Honolulu, Harris stumbled upon a spool of discarded telephone cable and considered it something of a miracle.

"Right in front of the post office was this underground cable, laying in the middle of the sidewalk," he recalls. "I thought, 'This is incredible.' Then I looked at it, and you could see all these different colors through the cut in the copper."

He borrowed a hack saw and cut through the cable's copper and plastic coating. Underneath a final layer of tar, he found the pot of gold, or, more accurately, a rainbow—strands of thin flexible wire insulated in 25 vibrant colors.

Intrigued by his discovery, Harris tried twisting and bending pieces of the colored wire. The activity proved more than just good exercise for his crippled left hand.

"I had quite a lot of pain in the healing process of learning how to use my hand again. Every time it would hurt, I'd just pick up the wire and work with it, and I wouldn't think any more about the pain. I would be thinking about the wire. So actually it was therapeutic, because it took my mind off me."

Harris began to experiment with the wire, weaving it into a flexible, tight-knit mesh. He took it a step further and created a multicolored headpiece he called "The Crown of Hearts," because it was decorated in front with a large valentine.

Pleased with his eye-catching work, he made other things, including a chest ornament and matching skirting. He sold those two items for scrap copper one morning when he was desperately hungry for breakfast. But he wouldn't part with the crown and even mailed it to his father, back on the mainland, for safekeeping.

It may have been the end of the wire Harris found in Honolulu, but it was only the beginning of his career as an artist. Before he could continue, though, he had some experiences so troubling he decided to leave Hawaii.

"I was seeing things, like aliens," Harris says. "I saw people that did not seem all human. It was in one of the missions. There were these missionaries, and I talked with them, and they grew antennas and horns. I watched them grow right in front of me. It blew my mind. That's why my dad helped me come to the mainland. I was just freaking out."

Harris's parents, by then, had been divorced for years. His father, a career military man, had settled in Mobile, Alabama, after retiring from the service. He gave Harris enough money to travel to Mobile, and in 1982, Harris moved in with his father. Although he didn't get a paying job, Harris quickly found tasks to keep him busy. A trained landscaper and house builder, he volunteered to help repair damage wrought by Hurricane Frederick.

80

David Chesley Harris   12/17/93   Mobile, Alabama

He also began visiting scrap yards, looking for more of the colorful telephone wire. Soon, he was once again twisting the stuff into a variety of sculptures, including animals, flowers, masks, and headdresses.

Although not all his pieces can be worn on the head, he calls most of them crowns. "Everything you do in life is a crowning achievement," he explains. "That's why I call it a crown. It's another word for achievement."

Harris initially displayed much of his art in the library of the Baptist church he had joined. But he soon met a local gallery owner who began selling Harris's work and introducing him to other people in the Mobile arts community.

"I was very shy," Harris says. "It was very difficult for me to communicate with someone, to talk to them at length. I think that's why I was allowed to have the gift to do this. When I finished one (sculpture), someone would ask me to explain it to them, and it got easier and easier."

Harris started calling himself "Sir Chesley," a title that was hard to ignore. The moniker combined his middle name with the polite salutation he was accorded as soon as he settled in the South.

"Everybody was calling me 'sir,' " he says. "I thought, am I that old? I looked up the word in the dictionary and saw that it was used to honor somebody who'd become a man. So I thought if everybody else calls me sir, I would too. My middle name is Chesley, and Sir Chesley had a nice ring to it."

Harris's work has been shown in local and national galleries, including the Smithsonian Institution. His recognition as an artist was another kind of crowning achievement for the Oklahoma native and eighth-grade dropout, whose childhood had hardly been typical or easy.

The third of ten children, he attended schools in a half dozen states as the family followed his father to military posts in the Midwest and Southeast. His family was living in Detroit in 1967, when the daily racial tensions at school became too much for young David to bear. He quit going to class and eventually was sent to a special boys camp, where he learned vocational skills, including landscaping and cooking.

During the 1970s, Harris worked as a gourmet chef in Detroit and Houston. In 1979, while riding his motorcycle in Houston, he collided head-on with a car that had turned unexpectedly in front of him. It was the first in a long string of mishaps that slowed down once he got to Alabama but never entirely stopped.

In 1990, Harris fell down a flight of stairs, injuring his back. And in September 1993, a stranger attacked Harris and some friends as they played pool in downtown Mobile. Harris ended up hospitalized and in a coma. Since his release from the hospital, his health has not been good.

Never married, he lives alone in a trailer and gets by on Social Security payments and the occasional sale of his wire creations. Harris has completed about 250 wire-mesh pieces, including a series of brightly colored robots he calls The Rainbow Saints.

He is also a prolific painter, having produced more than 5,000 paintings since he arrived in Mobile. "I never really get too deep with it," he says of his paintings, often colorfully playful abstracts. He hopes one day to publish his autobiography, along with examples of his artwork.

For all of his bad luck, Harris feels blessed. "I've had it rough, but at the same time, I've had it great. Because every time I'd finish a sculpture, there was a celebration. And I'm sure that's what's helped carry me through."

Mythical Creature, *1991.*
Telephone wire, door knob. Dimensions: 16" h.
Collection of Tut and Harry Riddick.

DAVID CHESLEY HARRIS

84

Crown of Glory, *1985.*
Telephone wire. Dimensions: 13 ½" h.
Fine Arts Museum of the South, Mobile, Alabama.

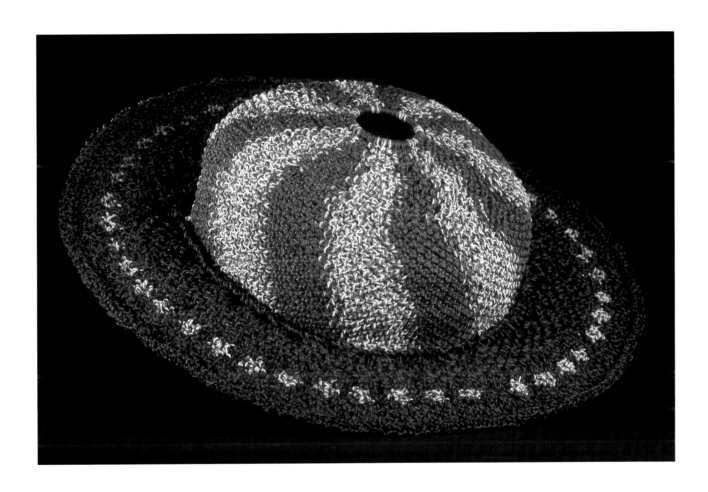

Crown of Independence, *1990.*
Telephone wire. Dimensions: 4 1/4" h.
Collection of Tut and Harry Riddick.

LONNIE BRADLEY HOLLEY

**Born February 10, 1950, in Birmingham, Alabama
Lives in Birmingham**

s a National Guard jet roars low across the sky, Lonnie Holley stands at a rickety table in his backyard, giving his visitors an impromptu art lesson.

"Give me your mind for a minute and let me show you how to do something beautiful with it," he says to one visitor. Holley then reaches into a large black portfolio, pulls out a foot-long scrap of yellowed drawing paper, and gently sets it in the middle of the table.

Next he picks up a small paint brush and dips it into a bucket of blue house paint. Waving the brush over the paper, he watches the paint drip into globs of blue. From under the table, he pulls out small jars of acrylic paint and repeats the dripping process until the old drawing paper is similarly streaked with purple, yellow, gold, red, and green.

"Now let's watch this become beautiful," he says. Holley takes another piece of drawing paper and presses it gently onto the first sheet. After a couple of seconds, he pulls the sheets apart and sets them on the table, side by side. "Now isn't that beautiful," he says in a soft, childlike voice. "Once I get the paint down, I can see what this piece has to offer me."

Holley's young children, playing in the yard with friends from the neighborhood, walk quietly to the table. Entranced, they watch the artist, who strikes a colorful figure with his hair in dreadlocks, rings on nearly every finger, and beaded bands around his wrists and ankles.

Holley uses another brush to add swirling, large-lipped profiles to his matching new abstracts. When finished, the pieces suggest an African-inspired Madonna and child.

"This is 'The Purpose and the Reason,' " Holley announces, as the finished paintings lie drying on the table.

The mother in the first picture, he explains, is the reason for the existence of the child, or the mother's purpose, in the second picture.

"I'd like to see love in this manner," Holley says softly, almost to himself. "I'd like to see the family come back together."

The importance of family, and especially children, is a major theme in Holley's paintings, found-object assemblages, and sandstone sculptures. The works fill to overflowing his one-acre homestead near the Birmingham International Airport in Birmingham, Alabama.

Holley's yard, in fact, is perhaps his greatest work of art—a shady maze of old kitchen appliances, junked cars, clothes, beat-up furniture, farming tools, and machine parts festooned with Christmas lights, artificial flowers, and even a bit of yellow police tape that reads, "Crime scene. Keep out."

"The average person can't understand this," Holley says. "But a lot of people say, 'Good night. You made me think.' If you look at all this thrown-away material, I took it and made it into something else. But it took that creative effort. It was already created. It was already at point A. When you throw it away, I'll take it from point A to the next level."

He stops below a piece of rotting wood hanging by a wire from a backyard tree. "That piece of driftwood offers a lot," Holley says. "It tells a lot about what someone else could see in something. This piece of driftwood can be looked at as a gun, as a shooting arrow, as some kind of space-age material."

He leads the way to another display—a dirty black doll tied to a dilapidated chair. An ordinary yard rake, in seemingly good condition, has been wired to the back of the chair.

Lonnie Holley   6/6/93   Birmingham, Alabama

The piece is titled "Don't Use Her For A Rake Or Hoe." "I don't think young children should be looked at like that," Holley says. "They should be allowed to develop, not just be tied up."

Holley's concern for children probably goes back to his own troubled childhood. As he talks about those days, Holley begins to cry. The tears streak down his smooth brown cheeks.

His mother, he says, gave him away when he was an infant. Or rather, he corrects himself, another woman took him and never gave him back. The woman, whose name he can't remember, carried him to Ohio, then brought him back to Birmingham and sold him to a woman bootlegger for a pint of whiskey when he was four years old.

Five years later, after the bootlegger was dead and Lonnie could no longer tolerate her abusive husband, he climbed on top of a train at Birmingham's old Terminal Station and rode it all the way to New Orleans.

He eventually ended up at a New Orleans juvenile detention facility, and, finally, at the Alabama Industrial School for Boys and Girls at Mount Meigs. He lived there until he was 14 years old, when his natural grandmother brought him back to Birmingham to live with her family.

Here, the teenaged Lonnie got acquainted with his unmarried mother, Dorothy Mae Holley, who, by the time she died at age 69, had given birth to 27 children. He learned that his father was a house painter named A. J. Bradley. (Holley eventually took his father's surname as his middle name.)

With his poor reading and writing skills and lack of social grace, Holley found public school intolerable. He dropped out with just a seventh-grade education and went with his brother to Orlando, Florida, where they found jobs working in a country club. For a time, Lonnie helped maintain the golf course, then was promoted to dishwasher and, finally, to cook.

After working as a chef in Disney World and several Orlando restaurants, Holley returned to Birmingham in the mid-1970s and took a job at a breakfast restaurant. "I still know how to cook forty-eight different pancakes," he says. "I learned how to flip pancakes two skillets at a time."

By the time he returned to Birmingham, Holley had fathered ten children, all in Florida, and all without benefit of marriage. "I was a lover," he says, smiling. "I think I'm still a lover, but I don't chase ladies like I used to. I prefer to do my work and grow my children that I already have."

Back in Birmingham, Holley lived with relatives and eventually got married, but his life remained far from stable. He drank wine, smoked marijuana, and went into a deep depression. "I thought maybe my life wasn't worth nothin' to nobody, and I thought about committing suicide. That's when the sandstone came into my life."

Holley and his wife, Carolyn, were living near a pipe manufacturing plant, where the grounds were littered with sand and clay slabs, a by-product of the steel industry. Holley had accumulated a small collection of the material by 1978, when his sister's children were killed in a house fire. The family had no money for tombstones, so Holley used kitchen utensils to carve the children's names into pieces of sandstone, which he placed at their graves.

Soon he was making more tombstones, peddling them from door to door. Business hardly boomed, and Holley began experimenting with the sandstone. He first carved simple Indian figures, but was soon creating complex carvings depicting Jesus Christ, Dr. Martin Luther King, Jr., Birmingham Mayor Richard Arrington, and President John F. Kennedy.

"A lot of people said, 'That ain't gonna get you nowhere,'" Holley recalls. "But this one old lady told me I ought to take my pieces to town, instead of waiting for town to come to me."

In the Beginning, God Created, *1984.*
Acrylic on paneling. Dimensions: 48" x 12 3/16".
Collection of Robley M. Hood.

In 1979, Holley carried eight of his sculptures to the Birmingham Museum of Art, where an astonished Richard Murray, then museum director, took the artist under his wing. Besides displaying Holley's work in the museum, Murray introduced him to benefactors and also brought his carvings to the attention of the Smithsonian Institution, which featured Holley's work in its "More Than Land And Sky (Art of the Appalachia)" touring exhibition.

Holley concentrated on his sandstone sculptures and began selling them to collectors. He kept his favorites, including a large self-portrait and "A Baby Being Born," a sculpture he carved when his wife was pregnant with their second child.

By the mid-1980s, Holley had started painting but was too embarrassed to show the work to his friends or the art dealers who visited. One Birmingham friend, Robley Hood (now a teacher in New Orleans), finally spied Holley's pictures and was thrilled by the work. Encouraged, Holley began to spend more time on his paintings and his growing collection of junk, which he turned into environmental sculptures.

To supplement money earned from the sale of his art, Holley makes presentations at schools, churches, and arts festivals, where he's especially popular with young children, who call him "The Sand Man."

Holley knows a lot about entertaining children. Since 1987, he has been a single father to his and Carolyn's five young children while Carolyn serves a prison sentence for armed robbery in Ohio. As Holley puts it, "She was in the wrong place at the wrong time." He and the children visit her in prison once a year.

By the time Carolyn gets out of jail, Holley expects his family will have been forced to move from their house in Birmingham's Airport Hills because of an airport expansion project. If they do relocate, Holley plans to take his unique environment with him.

That he is a professional artist, to Holley, is nothing short of a miracle. It has allowed him to express himself, to earn a living, and to find purpose in the things people throw away, including human beings.

"I got an opportunity to recycle, in a sense, my own innerness," he says. "People say, 'What a difference a day makes.' But to me, what a difference a second makes, or an hour, when you're doing something positive with a mind."

Don't Grow Him Up Green, *1991.*
Oil and paper on paper. Dimensions: 36" x 25".
Collection of Robley M. Hood.

LONNIE BRADLEY HOLLEY

92

Life Must Pass On, *1983.*
Industrial sandstone. Dimensions: 12" h.
Robert Cargo Folk Art Gallery, Tuscaloosa, Alabama.

A Positive and a Negative in the Womb of Life, *1991.*
Acrylic on paper. Dimensions: 36" x 34".
Collection of Rena Selfe.

94

Supporting the Heart, *1992.*
Wood, metal, straw, fabric, cord, string, nylon. Dimensions: 25" h.
Collection of William Arnett.

Crucifix of Hunger, *1993.*
Fabric, plastic, metal, rubber on wood. Dimensions: 40" h.
Collection of William Arnett.

BOOSIE JACKSON

Born 1881 in Union Springs, Alabama
Died 1966 in Alabama

In a March 1952 edition of *The Montgomery Advertiser*, an uneducated mason and house builder named Boosie Jackson explained his plans to create a wooden zoo. "I'm going to have all types of things in it, lions, elephants, zebras, monkeys, everything," he told reporter Joe Azbell. "I always dreamed of owning a zoo."

The article detailed how "the 70-year-old Negro" already had turned his Union Springs, Alabama, home into a tourist attraction by painting a Noah's ark-like menagerie of animals onto a stone wall beside his house.

By the time he died in 1966, Jackson had fulfilled his dream. His front yard was a wonderland of his homemade animals, fashioned from concrete left over from the tombstones he built and sold from his home. There were bigger-than-life alligators, serpents, and birds surrounding a concrete milk pitcher almost as tall as the house. "There was also a sign that said, 'Rocks of Ages, all works built by Boosie Jackson,' " recalls Montgomery artist Anton Haardt. She first visited Jackson's beloved zoo in 1972, only days before the long-condemned property was bulldozed to the ground on orders from the city.

Ms. Haardt had heard about Jackson's unique environment from a fellow artist. After learning it was about to be destroyed, she tried unsuccessfully to get area universities interested in salvaging Jackson's work. So the day before the demolition crew was scheduled to arrive, she returned to the property in her pickup truck and managed to save a few items from the house and yard.

"I was just overtaken by how interesting the whole menagerie was," Ms. Haardt says. "It was incredible to see a milk pitcher that was ten feet high in front of somebody's house. There was also a saucer the size of a child's swimming pool. I went in the house, and it was how they had left it. There were bedspreads on the beds, but the rats had eaten everything, and the floors were torn up and the ceilings were falling in. There was a brass bed in the front room, and furniture inside. And I remember an old glass cabinet."

Among the items Anton Haardt took was a painting by Jackson and a matching hand-carved frame. "I paid the lady next door five dollars for everything I got, so that at least some-

Photo courtesy Anton Haardt.

96

This Is French African Bilding (sic), *ca. 1950-1960.*
Paint and pencil on composite board. Dimensions: 36" x 52½".
Collection of Anton Haardt.

body got paid for something," Ms. Haardt says. The concrete pieces were too heavy to remove.

But days later, after the bulldozers had done their damage, Ms. Haardt returned and salvaged a few broken pieces, including the little cement bird that had been poised on top of the giant milk pitcher.

Years later, when she organized an exhibit of outsider art that would include the pieces salvaged from Jackson's home, Ms. Haardt began to research the life of the artist.

His Union Springs neighbors—at least the few who could remember him—told how Jackson would walk up the street carrying his hammer and a measuring stick in a sack over his shoulder. He liked to tell the local boys that "if you aren't good, I'll put you in this sack and throw you in my wishing well. That's where I keep bad kids."

Jackson was a big man who, despite having never attended school, seemed relatively cultured and sophisticated, and clearly proud of his African heritage. He married, had at least one child, and earned his living building houses and tombstones. In his spare time he painted pictures, many with African motifs, and molded his concrete critters. He also carved wooden utilitarian items, such as walking canes, ax handles, and washboards.

After the concrete pieces were demolished, Anton Haardt was able to see how Jackson made them. "He did it with metal grids, wires, and nails," she says. "I think what he did was dig these molds into sand, then he poured in the concrete, put in the metal supports, poured more concrete, in and then let it dry."

Jackson received a brief flurry of attention in the 1960s, when a Broadway actress named Helen Claire learned about him during visits in Union Springs, her hometown. She even arranged for an exhibition of his work at Tuskegee Institute.

Not until Ms. Haardt included his work in her "Orphans in the Storm" exhibition in the late 1980s did Jackson receive further recognition. Indeed, from what he told *The Montgomery Advertiser* in 1952, Jackson remained largely unappreciated in his hometown.

He described to the newspaper how a group of white boys had stopped by his house and borrowed his earliest homemade wooden and concrete animals for some sort of parade, and how the boys never came back. "They just kept my whole zoo," Jackson said. "I am going to build me another, and I ain't loaning this one out no more."

Anton Haardt says nobody could have borrowed the animals she found adorning Jackson's house in the days before the bulldozers came. "They must have weighed at least five hundred pounds apiece," she says. "It would have taken a forklift to move them."

Soldier, *ca. 1950-1960.*
Paint on wood. Dimensions: 36" h.
Collection of Anton Haardt.

RONALD LOCKETT

Born May 20, 1965, in Bessemer, Alabama
Lives in Bessemer

"Come out here," Ronald Lockett says, leading the way outside the dirt-floor garage that serves as his art studio. "I want to show you something funny."

There, etched into the metal outer wall of the dilapidated garage, is the faint outline of a pair of images, drawn many years ago, when Ronald was just a boy. One shows a pig, etched into the metal by Lockett's father, Short. Underneath it is a dog, drawn by young Ronnie himself, all those years ago.

"I could always draw," Ronald says slowly in his soft-spoken, thoughtful manner. "I can remember when I was in the first grade, I drew something, I think it was a rhinoceros, and the teacher came up behind me, and she went and got another teacher to come look. She said, 'Look at that. He might be a great artist someday.' I'll always remember it. 'Cause it made me feel proud."

Lockett still lives in the same little gray house he's lived in all his life, in a run-down Bessemer, Alabama, neighborhood known as Pipe Shop for its close proximity to a pipe manufacturing plant. Lockett's cousin, Thornton Dial, used to live just a few doors down until he became a famous artist and moved to an estate in the country.

It was Thornton Dial's initial success as an artist, in the mid-1980s, that encouraged Ronald to pursue his interest in painting and drawing. "I always wanted to be an artist, but the chance of me getting my work shown was slim and none," he says. "I hated to let it go, but reality was reality. And then, by fate, Mr. Bill Arnett showed up, and I had the opportunity to do a few things."

Arnett, the Atlanta art dealer and collector who befriended Thornton Dial and became his agent, has also helped Lockett sell his work and get it seen by the right people. One of Lockett's pieces, called "Darkest of Africa," sold for $9,000 a few years ago. "That was a big moment in my life," the artist says. "It's something I'm still very proud of."

But Lockett has yet to achieve the kind of stardom his cousin has enjoyed in recent years. Ronald still does his art in the old garage, which has no door and gets icy cold in the winter. Even in the frigid months, Lockett works on his paintings. He'll stay in the garage until his hands get numb, then go in the house a while to warm up, and then return to the garage to continue his work.

Many of his pieces comment on social issues, most often homelessness, hunger, and the environment. For a piece-in-progress, called "Famine," Ronald took a sheet of old, rusted metal and used a hammer and nails to carve an image of a woman holding her starving baby.

Many of his paintings, including a piece he's especially proud of called "Rebirth," incorporate a variety of objects, often bits of salvaged wire. Many works include images of wild animals; in "Traps," the animals are caught in a net, trying desperately to escape.

"My neighbor down the road, he kills deer, but I'm not a hunter," Lockett says. "It's something I feel strongly about. But I don't have no explanation about why my stuff turns out the way it is. There really ain't no reason. I just try to express my ideas."

In some ways, "Traps" may be a metaphor for Lockett's own life. One of five children, he was still a child in the mid-1970s when his parents' divorce caused his mother to have an emotional breakdown. As his mother tried to get her life back together, young Ronald looked after his siblings and took refuge in his art.

Ronald Lockett   12/23/93 Bessemer, Alabama

His talent was obvious even in grammar school, when his classmates would beg him to draw pictures for them to take home, especially during holidays. "In school, every kid in the class would hand me their paper to draw them a Christmas tree, or something for Halloween or Thanksgiving. I'd have to draw twenty-two or twenty-three of them. It was like I was the only person who could draw. I didn't have to do it, but I did."

Ronald did well in school-sponsored art contests. One of his favorite memories is of beating his best friend, a fellow artist, in one such competition. "He was good, a little better than I was," Ronald recalls.

"I didn't have any technique, and still don't. But I asked him would he teach me. He looked at me like I was crazy and said no. He said he couldn't teach me because I might get better than him. Then we got in this art contest, and I got second place and he got third. He came running up to me and said, 'I can't believe it. The judges must have made a mistake.' "

After graduating from Hueytown High School in 1984, Lockett began to drift, working odd jobs, with no focus on career or future. At one point, he contemplated joining the army, but a brother convinced him to concentrate on his art. (That same brother, a career army specialist named David Lockett, made international headlines in 1991, when he was taken captive and held prisoner in Iraq for weeks during the Gulf War. He was released unharmed.)

Inspired by Thornton Dial's creative use of junk, Lockett soon was scavenging for discarded objects he could incorporate into his art. His mother at first allowed him to paint in his room, but she didn't like the mess and eventually banished his work to the garage.

"It's a wonder I never caught the flu, working out in that cold," Lockett says. "I don't think my mother meant any harm. She just couldn't stand the paint fumes.

"Really, if I wouldn't have had so much adversity, I don't think I'd be doing this today. I think I would have just taken things for granted. When things were bad, I wanted to prove I could do this. I was just determined."

Deer, *1993.*
Painted tin, metal, nails on wood. Dimensions: 37 1/2" x 52".
Collection of William Arnett.

RONALD LOCKETT

Traps, *1993.*
Tin, netting, fabric, branches, oil on wood. Dimensions: 35 ¹/₂" x 56".
Collection of William Arnett.

Morning of Peace, 1988.
Oil, chicken wire, macrame on wood. Dimensions: 49" x 47".
Collection of William Arnett.

WOODIE LONG

Born October 10, 1942, in Plant City, Florida
Lives in Andalusia, Alabama

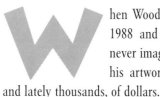hen Woodie Long picked up a brush in 1988 and painted his first picture, he never imagined he soon would be selling his artwork to collectors for hundreds, and lately thousands, of dollars.

On hiatus from his job as a house painter, he was home alone, reflecting on his life, and especially his childhood. He wanted to record those bittersweet memories, to make them real again. Because his spotty education had left him barely able to read and write, Long decided to draw his memories.

His wife, Dot, had left their Andalusia, Alabama, home that morning for her art class at nearby Lurleen B. Wallace State Junior College. But Dot–an accomplished watercolor artist–kept plenty of brushes, paints, and drawing paper in the house. Long dug through her art supplies and settled down at her desk to work. When his wife returned, Long had three finished paintings to show her.

"I had 'em outside on the swing," Long recalls. "I knew they was good. And it scared me to death. I just said, 'That's somethin'.' When Dot got here, she called her art teacher, and he came out and tried to buy 'em from me. I said I could probably get twenty dollars apiece for 'em. He said, 'I'll give you thirty dollars.'"

Each painting depicted colorfully outfitted, willowy black women rendered in crude, yet fluid brush strokes that made them seem alive and moving. As Long tells it, he was painting his aunts, as he remembered them from all those years ago. He painted them brown, he says, because he couldn't figure out how to paint white skin.

"I thought I had something special, and Dot did too. She's pretty hard to please when it comes to art. She thought I got lucky, I think. But then I started painting hundreds of 'em, even thousands now, and I just feel so comfortable."

Dot's art teacher, Lonnie Rich, recalls his initial response to Woodie's earliest artistic expression. "It was very crude, not in the negative sense, but in gut expression," Rich says. "That is very, very rare. It was very fluid–strictly emotion poured out on the canvas."

Long soon had his own supply of acrylic paints and art paper. He began turning out scores of pictures showing more of his childhood memories. He painted scenes of children tumbling atop a lumpy feather bed, farmers plowing with their mules, children flying kites and riding bicycles, and truckloads of farm boys heading down the road.

"I had wanted to write my memories down," Long says. "I had a lot to say, you know. But it was just too hard for me to do. I can talk a million miles an hour, but I can't write. So I thought, why don't I paint 'em?"

With encouragement from Dot and Rich, Long soon turned out enough of his memory paintings for a one-man show at the junior college. The locals who attended bought 36 of the 40 paintings on display. And Long, who signed each one with his nickname "Woodie," knew he had found a new and promising career.

In the five years since, Long has painted more than 6,000 pictures–on paper, wood, metal, and any other surface that strikes his fancy. At the annual Kentuck Festival of the Arts in Northport, Alabama, he quickly became the new darling of folk art collectors, who travel from as far away as New York and California to buy his pictures.

Dot has abandoned her own promising art career to serve as Woodie's full-time business manager. And it has turned into

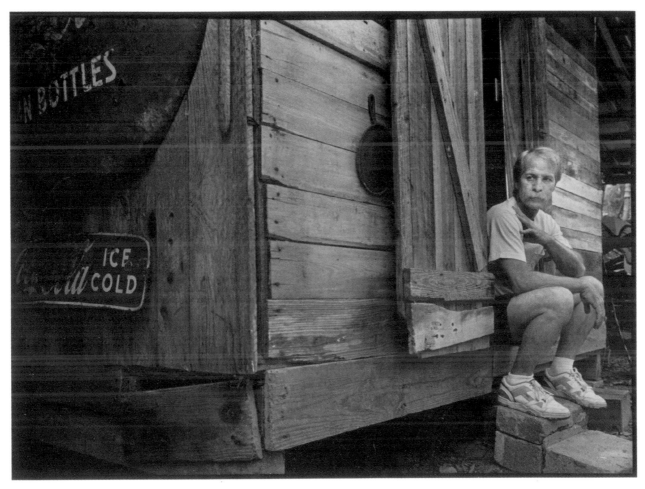

Woodie Long   7/10/93   Andalusia, Alabama

quite a task. "She's workin' on my taxes right now," Woodie says. "I told Dot I'm gonna quit paintin' 'cause Uncle Sam's eatin' me alive."

That he makes too much money wasn't, until recently, of concern to Long. Originally from Plant City, Florida, he was one of 12 children born to a hard-drinking sharecropper, who dumped his wife and children at a Tampa housing project before running off with another woman.

Although Woodie was a teenager when his daddy left, he could barely read or write. "Daddy didn't like us going to school," he explains. After studying hard in night classes, Long managed to finish high school at age 20.

During the next two decades, he got married and divorced twice, had two children and earned his living painting houses in the Tampa area and also overseas. In the mid-1970s, he traveled to Saudi Arabia to work as a painter for a construction company. There, he met Dot, an American whose parents worked for the U.S. Army Corps of Engineers.

In 1980, the two moved back to the states, where they bought a van and toured the country. They finally landed in Andalusia, where one of Woodie's sisters had lived for years.

There, Dot and Woodie—who wed in 1984—settled into a run-down cabin nestled in the woods on the outskirts of town. The house and four surrounding acres cost them $5,500.

While Dot attended art classes, Woodie continued to paint houses, though his back hurt and the paint fumes had started making him dizzy. By 1988, he decided he couldn't do the work anymore. And it was then that he sat down with Dot's acrylic paints and produced his amazing pictures.

"I knew from the start he'd be able to make a living with his work," says Dot, a tall, friendly woman, who—though 15 years younger than her husband—seems almost protective of

him. "I thought it was unique, special and very creative. I kind of wondered, too: Did he just get lucky? But he just kept getting luckier all the time."

From Woodie's success, the couple has been able to renovate their old house and even acquire a few "luxuries," such as kitchen appliances and air conditioning. They've expanded their vegetable garden to cover an acre. Right now, Woodie says, it's filled with carrots, radishes, lettuce, and collards.

The art studio in back of their house that Woodie built years ago for Dot is where he, not his wife, goes to paint nearly every day. Although he still paints his childhood memories, the scenes have grown increasingly complex and detailed.

He's been working hard on a series of pictures called "I Was Shot A Million Times Before I Was Seven Years Old." The paintings were inspired by his recollections of old movies and TV shows featuring cowboys and Indians.

He also has been painting sports scenes, including one called "The First Play Of The Game," which depicts the annual football showdown between the arch rivals University of Alabama and Auburn University. "It's really something," says Woodie, repeating one of his favorite phrases.

A small man with wispy graying blond hair and a matching mustache, Long exudes the wonder and innocence that define his paintings. He's endearingly boastful about his success. "It's something, to only be paintin' five and a half years, and you're one of the top sellers," he says.

In the next year or so, Long—who has been talking with publishers in New York—expects to see his illustrations gracing the pages of a children's book.

The appeal of his work, he says, is simple. "You can look at it and not have to figure out what in the hell's goin' on."

Grooming Willie, *1990.*
Acrylic on poster board. Dimensions: 6" x 9 1/4".
Artist's Collection.

110

Pregnant Sisters, *1990.*
Acrylic on poster board. Dimensions: 18 3/8" x 24 1/2".
Artist's Collection.

All Around the Mulberry Bush, *1990.*
Acrylic on poster board. Dimensions: 19 1/4" x 24 1/2".
Artist's Collection.

ANNIE LYKES LUCAS

Born February 18, 1954, in Autauga County, Alabama
Lives in Pink Lily community, Autauga County

When she was in the eighth grade, Annie Lykes Lucas had a science teacher who instructed his pupils to draw pictures of the different types of clouds they were reading about in their textbooks.

So she took her crayons and created images of billowy white masses floating against a heaven as pure and blue as the summer skies over rural Autauga County, Alabama, where she grew up.

Decades later, after she had married and given birth to six children, Annie would take up her crayons and paper and begin in earnest to draw and paint. And those same swirling clouds she had created in the eighth grade would turn up again and again, as a backdrop to the Biblical stories she would tell on canvas and cloth.

"I always liked to draw," Annie says, sitting in a garage-like art studio belonging to her husband, metal sculptor Charlie Lucas, behind the trailer they share in the Pink Lily community in Autauga County.

"In school, we had to draw the different clouds out of the science book," Annie says. "We had to draw animals— the different parts of their bodies. Then I started drawing large ships, but I did that on my own. I loved to draw ships and animals."

Before she finished the eighth grade, Annie answered an advertisement for lessons at an out-of-state art school. She wrote a letter, expressing interest in the training and the accompanying art supplies.

"One day a man came to the door, but when he saw how old I was, he told me to wait 'til I got out of school and then to write again," she recalls. "After that, I forgot all about it."

In those hard days, there wasn't much time to think about such things as art. Along with her father, mother, and most of her 14 siblings, Annie spent long hours picking beans in the fields north of Montgomery.

It was among the rows of beans that she met a sensitive young man named Charlie Lucas, who told her of his dreams of becoming an artist. When Charlie decided to look for a better life in Florida, Annie dropped out of the tenth grade and headed south to join him in Tampa, and they later married.

A few years later, when Charlie felt the need to return to Alabama, Annie followed him back home. They settled in Autauga County, on a few red-dirt acres dotted with trees and scrubby bushes. Always adept at making things, Charlie built them a house using scrap lumber. There, they set about raising their growing family.

In the mid-1980s, when Charlie injured his back cutting trees on his property, he had to give up any notion of returning to the manual labor jobs that had supported his family. During his recuperation, he began to explore his interest in art and his talent for making things out of junk.

Working a few hours each day, Charlie began to create outdoor metal sculptures out of automobile and bicycle parts

Photo courtesy Kentuck Museum.

The Seven Trumpets of Revelations *(Tryptic), ca. 1990.*
Acrylic, thread, glitter on broadcloth with batting backing. Dimensions: 40" x 40".
Collection of Georgine and Jack Clarke.

and other salvaged materials. He also began to paint pictures with house paint on wood and canvas boards.

Inspired by Charlie's art, Annie soon felt the urge to start drawing again. A devout Christian, she began to draw the stories she had read in the Bible. Especially interested in the Book of Revelation, she used acrylic paints and poster board to translate the apocalyptic words into colorful pictures.

"Revelations was the first thing I did," Annie says. "I just started, you know, from the back of the Bible. It was talking about the beasts and the devil, and I could just see in my mind how it was supposed to be, and I just started drawing."

In a series of seven pictures, she drew and then painted what she had read in Revelations—scenes of seven-headed beasts, of locusts swarming out of the ground, and of angels wrestling with the devil. Before drawing each picture, she would turn to the Book of Revelation and read verse after verse, searching for inspiration.

"I didn't understand it at first, and I had to read it over and over. The beasts represent a lot of things in the Bible. And it even talks about some of the things that's happening now."

One night in 1987, Annie prayed that God would show her a new and better way to express her devotion in her paintings. "I went to bed, and I seen a picture of Jonah and the Whale in my head. And the next day, I started working the thread and the cloth. It just came to me when I prayed."

Instead of merely painting her pictures, Annie begin to sew some of the images in her paintings. Working on canvas and fabric, she first drew her pictures and outlined the prominent images using thread and needle.

She then made bigger stitches with heavier thread to color in important characters. For some pieces, Annie worked with batting to raise the images off the material. The canvas or cloth was then stretched tightly across a wooden frame, which allowed her to complete the picture with her acrylic paints.

"That's how I do all my pieces now," Annie says. "If someone was blind, they could feel of it. Anytime I do my work, it's just like the picture's in front of me, and I can see it. When I start sewing, I can't wait to get through to see how it's going to look. When I tell myself I'm going to use a certain color, it comes to me when I'm working, and it's always a different color."

Annie usually works late at night in the trailer where she and Charlie live, across the street from the house Charlie built for his family in 1975. The house is now occupied by the couple's children, who range in age from 15 to 22. Annie and Charlie decided a few years ago that they could live and work better in the relative quiet of the nearby trailer.

Annie kept her original Revelations paintings, which took her years to complete. But she soon painted other scenes from the Book of Revelation, which quickly sold to collectors who discovered her work in the late 1980s.

Not all of her paintings are inspired by Revelations, but all can be traced to the Bible. She has painted and stitched the baptism of Jesus, Moses dividing the Red Sea, the destruction of Sodom and Gomorrah, and the confrontation between David and Goliath.

Two of her larger paintings hang on the ceiling in Charlie's studio. One, called "The Day the Devil Cast Out of Heaven," depicts seven-headed red dragons battling angels high in the clouds of a vivid blue sky.

"I'm glad peoples gets a chance to see my work and understand what I'm doing," Annie says. "A lot of people see it, and they don't believe it's in the Bible. So they go to the Bible and then they read about it. So I feel like God's working through me."

The Seven Trumpets of Revelations *(Tryptic), ca. 1990.*
Acrylic, thread, glitter on broadcloth with batting backing. Dimensions: 36" x 42".
Collection of Georgine and Jack Clarke.

116

The Seven Trumpets of Revelations *(Tryptic), ca. 1990.*
Acrylic, thread, glitter on broadcloth with batting backing. Dimensions: 20" x 33 ½".
Collection of Georgine and Jack Clarke.

Noah's Ark, *1992.*
Acrylic, thread on broadcloth. Dimensions: 17" x 23".
Cottonbelt Gallery / Micki Beth Stiller, Montgomery, Alabama.

CHARLIE LUCAS

Born October 12, 1951, in Birmingham, Alabama
Lives in Pink Lily community, Autauga County

As a cold winter rain pounds loudly on the tin roof of his backyard studio, Charlie Lucas sits beside an old wood-burning stove, trying to explain himself and his art.

"When I was a kid, I made toys out of metal or anything I could find. To me, when I walk around and look at stuff, it's almost like popcorn in a boiler. All of it's exciting. It's movin', it's jumpin', it's makin' up a noise to me."

His unique vision of "stuff" has allowed Lucas to take items that other people throw away and turn them into the whimsical metal sculptures that decorate his yard and have earned him acclaim in the folk art world.

Scattered about his property in rural Autauga County, Alabama, are scrap metal sculptures of dinosaurs, horses, birds, and even an airplane, complete with a scrap metal pilot. One of the largest pieces, called "Old Big Horse," is made from fence wire and steel bands and rises twelve feet off the ground.

Another sculpture, "Crazy Old Bird," also made out of metal bands, is perched on a steel post mounted in the ground. Nearby is the "Baby Dinosaur," reared back on its two hind feet. Life-size metal men, made from automobile parts, stand guard throughout Lucas's yard and adjoining acreage, where the scrubby brown grass grows in patches on the hard red dirt.

Parked in the middle of a field is the rusty metal airplane that Lucas calls "The Navigator." One of Lucas's earliest metal sculptures, it is named for its little pilot, whose head Lucas fashioned from an old bicycle seat, with the two coiled springs serving as the little man's protruding eyes.

Most of the sculptures incorporate metal banding–long metal strips often used in the packing and shipping of lumber. Lucas especially likes working with the strips, because he can weave them together in much the same way his grandfather wove baskets when Charlie was a boy.

"I wanted the weaving technique to be in my work," Lucas says. "That way, I can give the old ancestors the respect for what I learned from them. I use the old wheels a lot in honor of my great-grandfather, because he worked on wagon wheels and stuff. I had to make sure I could see them peoples again and again in my life, that I could look back and appreciate what they have did for me."

Born in Birmingham, Alabama, Charlie was the fifth of 14 children. His father was a mechanic, and his mother spent long hours picking beans in the fields of rural Elmore County, Alabama, where the family had settled.

As a boy, Charlie was often left in care of his younger brothers and sisters. He also helped his father work on car engines, learning the names of the tools and how the engine parts fit together. He spent his free time watching his grandfather weave baskets or learning the blacksmithing trade from his great-grandfather.

Although money was scarce and times were hard, Charlie's parents treated their children to family outings that made a lasting impression on a poor country boy. "I remember when my Mom and Dad was real young, they'd put us all in the

Photo courtesy Kentuck Museum.

Camel, *ca. 1985.*
Railroad spikes and found metal. Dimensions: 12" h.
Robert Cargo Folk Art Gallery, Tuscaloosa, Alabama.

car and take us for a nice ride, and we could see the towns, and it was better than buying us gifts and stuff," Lucas says.

"We'd drive up to Birmingham, and it was like drivin' halfway around the world. You lookin' at all the big trucks and stuff like that. I'd get in the back and just look at all this stuff. And sometimes I'd go to sleep, it would get that good."

The family had no money to buy toys, so Charlie learned to make his own. Using salvaged metal, wood, rope, and fabric, he made wagons, whirligigs, toy cars, and puppets. "It was better than waiting 'til Christmas to get a brand new toy," he recalls. "You could just build it and have it there to play with."

Yet his siblings weren't always impressed with Charlie's homemade toys. Because he wasn't interested in playing baseball and football with the other children, Charlie felt like an outcast at home and in school.

"I think I got into a lot of trouble 'cause what I did was always different from what my sisters and brothers did. To me, I was the bad apple in the barrel in some respects, because I didn't agree with anything they did. I couldn't see runnin' after no ball. I could maybe go out and watch them playing and maybe draw something on the ground. I was doin' my own thing. And I been doin' that all my life."

Charlie went to schools in Elmore and Autauga counties, but attended classes infrequently. Often he and the other Lucas children had to miss school to work in the fields. Charlie found it hard to catch up after months away from the classroom and ended up dropping out after the fourth grade.

Feeling out of place and misunderstood, "I kind of walked away from my family," he says. "I went and lived in the streets, all over. I just rode from town to town, hitch-hiking and stuff. I learned bricklaying, building on houses, digging in the flower beds, whatever kind of job I could get."

He worked construction all over the Montgomery area, learning enough about house building to promise himself he would one day build a house of his own. That was a promise he also made to Annie Lykes, the quiet young woman who had been special to him since they met as children in the fields of Autauga County.

When Charlie moved to Tampa, Florida, in 1968, he sent for Annie, and they got married. Although he had a good job and was happy in Florida, he was drawn back to Alabama. In 1971, the couple returned to Autauga County, where Charlie again went to work in the fields.

By 1975, he had earned enough money to buy property in the Pink Lily community near Prattville. There, using wood from old shipping crates and garage doors, he built a house for his family, which soon grew to include six children.

For several years, Lucas had a full-time job doing general maintenance work at a hospital in Prattville. After he was laid off in the early 1980s, he began clearing trees off his property, where he planned to build a workshop. But in 1984, while loading trees in the back of his truck, he fell and hurt his back.

"I walked home and told Annie I was hurtin' real bad," he recalls. "I laid down. And the next morning, I got up, and I couldn't walk."

During a long period of recuperation, Charlie began tinkering around his yard, making things out of scrap metal, just as he had done as a boy. "I think God slowed me down enough that I could open my mind up and maybe see myself as being a kid again," he says.

He took old railroad spikes and welded them together to make humpback camels. He picked up thrown-away car parts and welded them into life-size characters he set up in front of his house, like some peculiar welcoming committee.

These Are the Brothers, *1989.*
Wire and copper tubing. Dimensions: 20" h.
Robert Cargo Folk Art Gallery, Tuscaloosa, Alabama.

As he grew stronger, he began to build even larger pieces, such as the horses and dinosaurs and the little airplane he parked in the field at the center of his property.

Charlie began to call himself the "Tin Man," partly because he worked with metal and tin, but also because he had only $10 in his pocket when he realized that God had given him a new calling in life as a metal sculptor.

His work caught the attention of a Prattville newspaper, which printed a profile of the "Tin Man" and his unusual creations. Soon, dealers and collectors began to drop by the Lucas home, where, by the mid-1980s, Annie Lucas was discovering her own talent as a painter.

"I see it as something to play with, but in society, people call it art, this outsider thing," Charlie says of his work. "They say you's in the primitive art, you's in the folk art, you's in the outsider art. All these names come across me, and I don't know today what they talkin' about. I mean, maybe I'm all them wrapped up into one. It confused me. Maybe it's something you have to put on a person 'cause of the environment he lives in, or 'cause he didn't go to college. But I don't see it."

Many of Charlie's finest pieces still decorate his property, including at least 20 sculptures-in-progress. Some take months, and even years, to complete. He often starts a piece, works on it a few days, and then starts another piece. "That way, anytime I want to come out here and play with one of the toys, I got all the variety to play with. And I don't feel like I'm mass-producing the work."

He salvages much of the materials he uses from dumpsters or out of ditches at the side of the road. Friends and family bring him junked car parts and broken bicycles. Often, Charlie will be driving along and see a piece of junk that catches his eye and captures his imagination.

"When I go and look in some dumpster or ditch or somebody's backyard, the pieces go to talkin' to me. Sometimes I look at it and say, 'Do you want to go home with me? Will you be the thing that you say you will be?' Most times when I come home, the piece I done found will fit right into the piece I been working on for several years. I don't have to measure it or cut it. It just fits right in."

In recent years, Charlie has been concentrating, too, on his paintings–often playful scenes of animals and people, usually done in yellows, greens, reds, and browns. Through his art, he hopes to tell people "to be something for theirself, and to have God in front of you."

He believes Charlie Lucas himself has been recycled, along with the scrap metal pieces that go into his sculptures. "It's a long time you struggle with something, but when you see the value of yourself the struggle ain't near as bad. That's what I been tryin' to tell people. I went from being myself as nothin' in a way, and God has took my life and gave me a new name and a new meaning.

"I know it's a gift from God. Sometimes in your life, you never find the magic part of you. If you ever look for it, it won't be at the end of a rainbow. It'll be inside you. That will be your pot of gold."

And the Tin Man has one final message he wants delivered: "Tell the world that I love 'em," he says.

The Navigator, *ca. 1984.*
Metal bands and found metal objects. Dimensions: 64" h.
Artist's Collection.

124

The New Breed, *ca. 1990.*
Car springs, gears. Dimensions: 54" h.
Artist's Collection.

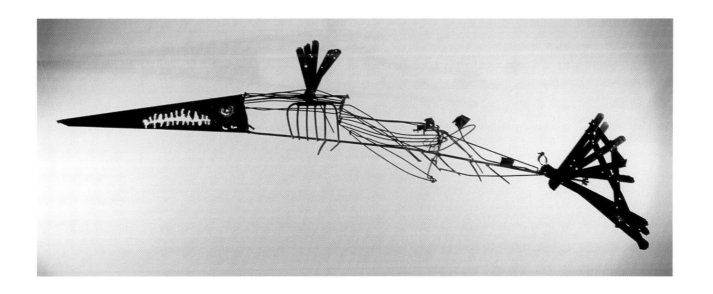

Little Willie, *1993.*
Found metal objects. Dimensions: 96" l.
Clary Sage Gallery, Birmingham, Alabama.

ROBERT MARINO

Born 1893 in Baldwin County, Alabama
Died 1973 in Daphne

Even as a boy growing up in South Alabama, Robert Marino was good with his hands, recalls his baby brother, Percy Marino, 88, who still lives in Daphne. "Robert had been carving along all his life," Marino recalls. "He'd go through the woods, and if he would see a tree or something interesting to him, he figured he could turn it into something worthwhile."

Before he died in 1973, Robert Marino turned his property into a sculpture garden, populated with his hand-carved wooden figurines. The first thing visitors saw, as they headed down the lane leading to his house, was a wooden horse head nestled in an oak tree.

Closer to the house stood a grinning replica of television star Andy Griffith, complete with a shock of hair made from a cow's tail. Nearby was a female character Marino called "Mary Ellen" after a woman who lived down the road. Hidden among the shrubbery was a carved likeness of Marino's favorite nephew wearing only a football helmet.

Beside the house stood a larger-than-life Indian woman with her two young children. Inside were more of his wooden characters, mostly replicas of famous figures of the 1960s– Nikita Khrushchev, Diahann Carroll, President John F. Kennedy, and Elvis Presley.

"He did mostly things he'd see on TV, whatever would appeal to him," says Percy Marino, who lives near his brother's old home and once shared his woodcarving hobby.

"He just took it up. He had always been handy with wood, and so was I. We just had the drive to do these things."

Originally from the community of Blacksher in northern Baldwin County, Robert Marino was the second of six children born to laborer Robert Marino and his wife, Eliza. While their

Photo courtesy Alabama Decorative Arts Survey.

126

Lighter Knot Bird, *ca. 1963-1973.*
Paint on wood. Dimensions: 6" h.
Fine Arts Museum of the South, Mobile, Alabama.

children were still young, the family moved south to Daphne to be near other relatives.

Percy Marino recalls an idyllic childhood and doting, loving parents. "My father and mother were both very dedicated people. We loved them both, and they were very good to us when we were coming up. We lived in the country, and that was good for children. I'd say our childhood was wonderful."

Robert completed high school in Daphne and set off for college at Tuskegee Institute. Before he could graduate, he was drafted to serve during World War I and spent 11 months stationed in France.

After the war, Marino returned to Daphne, where he married and had one child. A carpenter, he built his family a home and maintained a vegetable garden. He supported the family through his carpentry work, especially building houses.

Throughout his life Robert Marino made things out of wood—usually utilitarian items such as ashtrays, doorstops, and vases. When he reached his sixties and slowed down as a house builder, he began creating the wooden characters that decorated his property.

He began carving in earnest in the early 1960s, after a severe frost killed a camphor tree on his land. Marino made use of the unsightly tree by turning it into an oversized character.

He worked primarily with camphor, but he also used cedar, pine, cypress, and juniper—wood indigenous to Baldwin County. He painted many of his pieces to enhance their appearance and protect them from the elements.

Many of the characters were dressed in actual clothing—including "Mary Ellen," decked out in an antebellum dress complete with parasol. Marino clothed the figures, in part, to satisfy his wife, Vivian, who said she didn't want any naked people, wooden or otherwise, hanging around her property.

Although Marino was considered by some to be a recluse because he preferred to stay home and work alone on his carvings, he had many friends and could be outgoing if the occasion required it.

"He was mostly a quiet person, didn't have too much to say," Percy says. "He'd stay to himself. Most of the time, he worked on his own."

After Robert's death, his wife sold many of the wooden figurines. A selection of his work can be found in the Fine Arts Museum of the South in Mobile, Alabama.

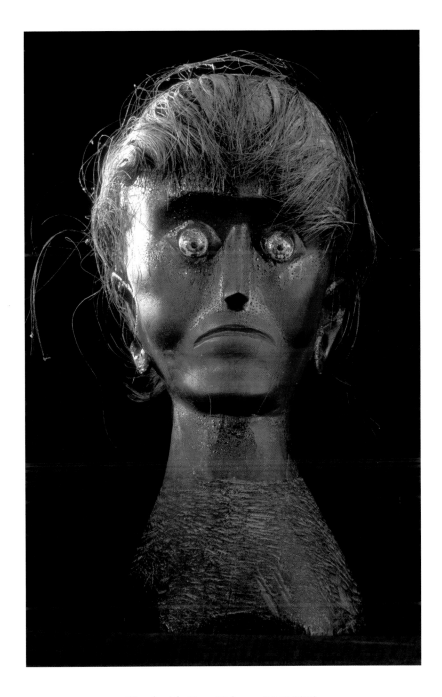

Head with Cow Hair, *ca. 1963-1973.*
Mixed media on wood. Dimensions: 10 ¼" h.
Fine Arts Museum of the South, Mobile, Alabama.

130

Mother and Child, *ca. 1963-1973.*
Ink on wood. Dimensions: 19" h.
Fine Arts Museum of the South, Mobile, Alabama.

Head with Crew Cut, *ca. 1963-1973.*
Ink on wood. Dimensions: 16" h.
Fine Arts Museum of the South, Mobile, Alabama.

SISTER GERTRUDE MORGAN

Born 1900 in Lafayette, Alabama
Died 1980 in New Orleans, Louisiana

Sister Gertrude Morgan was raised a Baptist, but, like Catholic nuns, she considered herself the bride of Christ. And she was a devoted, if eccentric, wife.

Beginning in the late 1950s and continuing until her death, she wore only white clothes, kept the inside and outside of her house painted white, and maintained the upholstery on her furniture in that purest of colors.

On the streets of New Orleans, the city where she had lived since the late 1930s, she was an untiring missionary who entertained potential converts with her preaching and singing, often to the accompaniment of her guitar or tambourine.

In her small frame house, which she called the "Everlasting Gospel Mission," she held regular prayer meetings and performed on her piano. The instrument, too, was painted white. To illustrate her often apocalyptic sermons, she painted pictures with the striking colors she steadfastly avoided in her wardrobe and home decor.

The Biblical Book of Revelation often inspired her paintings, such as "Christ Coming in His Glory," featuring a white-robed Jesus descending from the heavens. A giant eyeball stares from the center of "There Is An Eye Watching You," reminding sinners that God can see everything.

Another painting, "A Poem of My Calling," includes images of Sister Gertrude cleaning with a mop and strumming her guitar. It also features her handwritten narration–part biography and part statement of purpose:

"My heavenly father called me in 1934 on the 30th day of December or just about 38 years ago. The strong powerful words he said was so touching to me. I'll make thee as a signet for I have chosen thee go ye into yonders world and sing with a loud voice for you are a chosen vessel of mine to call men women boys and girls."

Born in Lafayette, Alabama, she lived for a time in nearby Columbus, Georgia, before heading for New Orleans in 1939, not long after her divine calling. She and two other women started an orphanage, which they supported through street collections.

Raised in the Baptist church, Sister Gertrude at first joined a fundamentalist sanctified sect that decreed its members dress entirely in black. It also emphasized communication with the Holy Spirit through music, song, and dance.

132

Chart of Revelations, *ca. 1965-1975.*
Acrylic and ink on paper. Dimensions: 22" x 28".
Collection of Kurt Gitter and Alice Yelen.

After Hurricane Betsy destroyed the orphanage in 1965, Sister Gertrude began preaching from her home. By then, she was dressing all in white, having received another divine message–that she was the bride of Christ.

In "A Poem of My Calling," painted in 1972, she recalled that story of grace. *"How I thank the Lord. He blessed this soul of mine. I did my mission work in the black robe around 18 years teaching holiness and righteousness that great work was so dear he has taken me out of the black robe and crowned me out in white. We are now in Revelation he married me I'm his wife the Lord of Hosts."*

If Sister Gertrude's mission in life was to save souls and preach the gospel, she also acquired a wide following among art collectors and others intrigued by her way of life and her colorful paintings.

Chicago folk art collector Susann Craig, who lived in New Orleans in the early 1970s, recalls visiting Sister Gertrude at her Everlasting Gospel Mission. "Everything in her house was white," Ms. Craig says. "The only color was in her paintings, in the pillows on the white chairs, and in her prayer robes."

Sister Gertrude's front yard, Ms. Craig recalls, was covered in four-leaf clover.

Ms. Craig met Sister Gertrude through gallery owner Larry Borenstein, who had befriended the artist and exhibited her work. Borenstein and another man, Alan Jaffe, tried to make sure Sister Gertrude had art supplies and enough money for the other things she needed.

"From what I could see, her needs were very limited," Susann Craig says. "The day I was there, her refrigerator had broken. They were going to send over another one, and Sister Gertrude said no, she wouldn't be needing a refrigerator, because the Lord had told her not to put anything colder than her body temperature in her mouth. I remember thinking, what a way to handle your problems."

Sister Gertrude sold her art through Borenstein's gallery and at local gatherings, including the New Orleans Jazz and Heritage Festival. In the early 1970s, her paintings were included in a show at the American Museum of Folk Art in New York City. Yet for all her artistic acclaim, Sister Gertrude clearly considered saving souls her primary calling.

Susann Craig recalls seeing the artist preaching on Royal Street in the French Quarter, where she would set up her paintings and address the small crowds that inevitably gathered. "She had this megaphone she made out of paper, and she would set up on the streets and preach from these pictures she had made on the Book of Revelation. She would use a steak bone as a pointer."

Sister Gertrude used some combination of acrylic paint, watercolor, crayon, pencil, and ink in most of her paintings, done primarily on cardboard, wood, and paper. Nearly all of her paintings were inspired by the Bible.

Many offered a short sermon. In "The Two Beasts of Revelations," she wrote, and no doubt believed, this wisdom from the Bible: *"Fear God and give glory to him: For the hour of judgement is come."*

Peter, James, and John, ca. 1974.
Acrylic, pen, and pencil on cardboard. Dimensions: 8 3/4" x 20 1/2".
Collection of Robley M. Hood.

The Harvest Is Ripe, *ca. 1973.*
Acrylic, pen, and pencil on cardboard. Dimensions: 7 1/8" x 8 1/16".
Collection of Robley M. Hood.

Spider Drake Driving Cows to the Butcher Pen, *ca. 1965-1975.*
Acrylic, pen, and pencil on paper. Dimensions: 11 1/2" x 15 1/2".
Collection of Susann Craig.

REVEREND BEN PERKINS

Born February 6, 1904, in Lamar County, Alabama
Died January 12, 1993, in Bankston

Reverend Benjamin Perkins had a philosophy about art, and it seemed to serve him well. "There's one thing I've learned," he told the *Birmingham Post-Herald* in a 1987 interview. "That is, people love the American flag. If you can get a church and a flag both on a thing, and you're not too high, then somebody'll buy it."

Whenever possible, Perkins put both an American flag and a little white church on his gourds and paintings, usually done in vibrant shades of red, white, blue, and gold, with touches of other bright colors. His gourds, and especially his paintings, often included Bible verses and Perkins's own bits of country-preacher wisdom, such as, "Go to church" and "Jesus is the answer."

Perkins began his art career in the early 1970s, when he built a little white church, like the ones in his paintings, on his

property in rural Fayette County, Alabama. With an artistic bent only partially satisfied by art classes at a nearby junior college, he soon began painting his favorite images and sayings on the front of the church, on his ramshackle house, and on anything else that would accommodate his brush.

In his house, which he built by himself in the 1970s, he kept an assortment of stuffed animals, souvenirs from his travels, and a dizzying array of his paintings and gourds. He began accumulating the hard-shell fruit after driving by a field of gourds during a trip through nearby Albertville.

As he told it, "I was coming down the number 75 highway, and I saw a bunch of gourds there, and I stopped and bought four. They were still green, and I had to wait 'til they dried, and after they dried, I thought, 'Well, why don't I paint 'em?' So I painted 'em, and from those four gourds, I got to where I am today."

Perkins's fondness for painting churches and flags reflected his background as a minister and retired marine. Born in rural Lamar County, Perkins grew up in the country, where his daddy was a farmer and holiness preacher. His mother died when he was a boy.

After attending public schools in Lamar and Fayette counties, young Ben Perkins joined the U.S. Marines at age 17 and set off to see the world. When his tour of duty ended four years later, he finished high school and enrolled at the University of Virginia, where he studied engineering and religion.

Ordained into the Church of God ministry, he became a part-time preacher, living in a number of states and working in a variety of jobs. He claimed to have studied Hebrew, driven a taxi, been a commercial fisherman, and worked for

Photo courtesy Kathy Kemp.

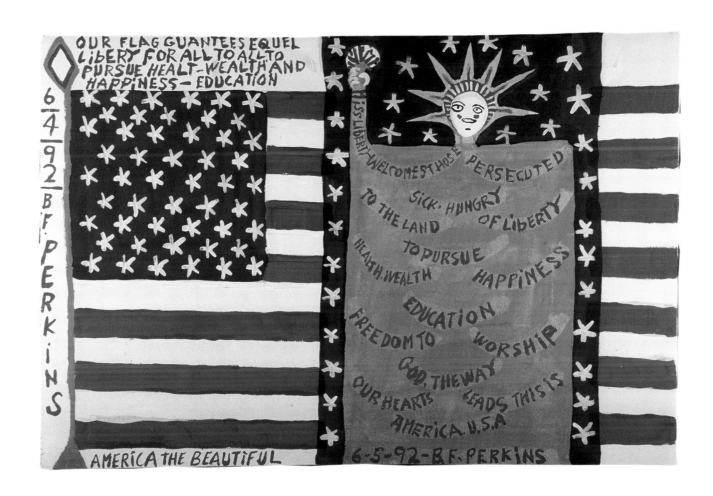

Flag and Statue of Liberty, 1992.
Acrylic on canvas. Dimensions: 24" x 36".
Gift to Fayette Art Museum, Fayette, Alabama, from Artist.

16 years as a safety engineer at National Airport in Washington, D.C.

Married, with two daughters, Perkins was living in Virginia when his wife took up with another man. "As long as she wasn't working, everything was all right," Perkins said. "But then she started working in a cafeteria, and she got a chance to talk to somebody else, and this fellow got his eye on her, got her to have coffee with him, got her to go to a show with him, and that was it."

After Perkins and his wife divorced, he stayed in Virginia long enough for his daughters to marry and start families of their own. In 1966 he returned to Alabama, settling at age 62 on 15 wooded acres in Fayette County, alone and lonely.

To keep busy, he built a house for himself, and then a church, which he called the Original Church of God. After a disagreement with the Church of God hierarchy, he broke away from the denomination and rechristened his church the Hartline Assembly Church of God, named after an old-time radio show called "Heartline."

Hurt by what he felt was mistreatment by church officials, Perkins erected a stone cemetery monument on his property. He had it engraved with these words: "I have only two hands and one life. I can not give more, will not give less. Benjamin F. Perkins."

After decorating his land with birdhouses, a gazebo, a fishing pond, and a replica of Jesus' tomb, Perkins began painting in earnest in the mid-1970s.

In his free time, he took art classes at nearby Brewer State Junior College. "I was afraid of lethargy," Perkins explained. "I did it to keep from sitting down and doing nothing. I wanted something to do when I got old."

Perkins kept a gourd patch on his property and supplemented his homegrown supply with frequent trips to Albertville. When he wasn't painting or taking art lessons, he kept busy attending meetings of the Fayette Chamber of Commerce and leading the local senior citizens exercise group.

And every Sunday, right up to his death, "Brother Ben," as Perkins was known to his many friends, held services in his little Hartline Assembly Church of God.

Since his death of a heart attack in early 1993, a handful of worshipers have continued to hold Sunday services in the Hartline church. But visitors are no longer free to wander about the property. The driveways are roped off and a sign has been posted on a tree near the house. "No trespassers," it reads in faded yellow letters. "Violators will be prosecuted."

Perkins's niece, Lois Sherrill, says the artist's daughters can't agree on what to do with Perkins's unique environment. So it sits there among the pine trees, empty and in need of repairs. The house, like the church, could use a coat of paint. The flags Perkins painted on the sides of the house have almost faded away. A padlock secures the front door.

If you look closely, you can still read the greeting Perkins painted in red letters on the door, always open to anyone. "The finest people on earth inters [sic] this door," it reads. "My friends—they are always welcome."

Cherokee Love Birds, *1992.*
Acrylic on canvas. Dimensions: 23 ½" x 18".
Gift to Fayette Art Museum, Fayette, Alabama, from Artist.

142

Perkins Home, *1992.*
Acrylic on canvas. Dimensions: 36" x 24".
Gift to Fayette Art Museum, Fayette, Alabama, from Artist.

Painted Gourds, *ca. 1984.*
Acrylic on dried gourds. Dimensions: 10" h, 20" h.
Robert Cargo Folk Art Gallery, Tuscaloosa, Alabama.

VIRGIL PERRY

Born February 19, 1930, in West Blocton, Alabama
Lives in Hueytown

One day, out of the blue, Virgil Perry's son-in-law brought him a peculiar gift–a cypress stump. A friend had given it to the son-in-law, and for a reason nobody seems to know, he thought Virgil ought to have it.

Another day, out of the blue, Virgil Perry's granddaughter looked at the cypress stump and asked him to carve her a unicorn. He didn't know much about carving or unicorns, but he figured he'd give it a try.

He carved up the stump, but there was no unicorn. So he got another cypress stump and tried it again. Still the unicorn did not appear. "I whittled away two or three of those stumps, and then I finally asked the Lord to show me this unicorn," Perry recalls. "And when I looked at the next stump, all I saw was that unicorn. When I carved it, it turned out great. So then I knew it was a gift from God."

The unicorn was the first of many wooden figurines Perry has carved in the seven years since he got that cypress stump from his son-in-law. Initially, Perry concentrated on making birds and fish, though he soon added people to his colorful menagerie.

Among them is his "Chinese Man" in a flowing red robe; his "French Man," who wears a green turtleneck and smokes a pipe; and his "Lady With the Beehive Hairdo," which doesn't need further description.

He carved a coal miner, complete with a tiny hardhat equipped with a battery-powered light, in honor of his coal mining son-in-law. Among his more recent pieces is his "Lady in an Evening Gown," who holds a single rose in her hand. Perry is particularly proud of her, because she's proof that he's getting better and better at carving faces. "I've got a nice face on that lady," he says.

Until he made that unicorn in 1987, Perry's carving had been limited to childhood whittling and, as an adult, a hobby making little wooden jellybean dispensers.

He spent his early years in West Blocton, Alabama, where his father was a coal miner and his mother a homemaker. When he was about 12, the family moved to the McCalla area and later to the Lipscomb-Brighton area west of Birmingham.

"As a kid," Perry says, "I whittled slingshots, staffs, stuff like that. But I probably didn't really know what a whittler was back then, if you want to know the truth."

Perry left school in the eleventh grade to join the air force, and he spent the next 21 years in the military, working as a personnel supervisor. He married a girl from back home, had four children, and lived for a dozen years in Washington, D.C.

After retiring from the air force in 1968, Perry returned to Alabama and settled in the Birmingham suburb of Hueytown. He embarked on a second career, as a clerk in a can company, where he worked until the company closed in 1980.

Not long afterward, a friend brought him a present from the World's Fair in Knoxville, Tennessee–a wooden jellybean dispenser. Perry promptly set about reproducing it in his workshop.

By the time his son-in-law handed him that cypress stump, Perry had made hundreds of jellybean dispensers and was, at least subconsciously, ready to move on to something that required more imagination.

Within a year, he'd carved enough animals to show at an arts and crafts fair in nearby Bessemer. There, he met a

Virgil Perry   10/25/93 Hueytown, Alabama

Birmingham folk art collector named Steve DeMedicis, who encouraged Perry to try carving people.

DeMedicis also helped Perry set suitably higher prices for his work and became an avid collector. "Steve introduced me to a lot of people interested in my work," Perry says. "I really owe my success to him." Perry was thrilled to be among the folk artists invited to craft ornaments for the 1993 White House Christmas tree. Using one of his trusty cypress stumps, he carved a flying angel.

Most mornings after breakfast Perry heads behind his house to his one-room shop, where he'll spend two or three hours working on his latest piece. He uses a pocketknife, wood rasp, jigsaw, and sandpaper. The more complex carvings often involve gluing on arms and accessories. Each piece is sanded, colored with acrylic paint, and then varnished. A single figurine usually takes three or four days to complete.

"It takes me a long time to make these things, but I'm in no hurry. I just sit out there and carve, have a good time and then come in the house. I don't try to make a job out of it."

While he's in his workshop, Perry's wife, Ruby, passes the time indoors with her library books. When Perry gets low on cypress stumps they head for Ozark, in south Alabama, where he buys a carload for up to $6 a stump.

He never knows what he's going to make until he looks at a stump and says his prayer. Although he's not much of a churchgoer, Perry believes he's seen the power of God firsthand.

"I believe my carving is a gift from God. I know it is. I sure do."

146

Sailor, *1987.*
Acrylic and varnish on cypress and driftwood, with sawdust, glue, string, and button eyes.
Dimensions: 8 1/2" h. Artist's Collection.

148

Man with Bird Walking Stick, *1991.*
Acrylic and varnish on cypress. Dimensions: 13" h.
Collection of Micki Beth Stiller.

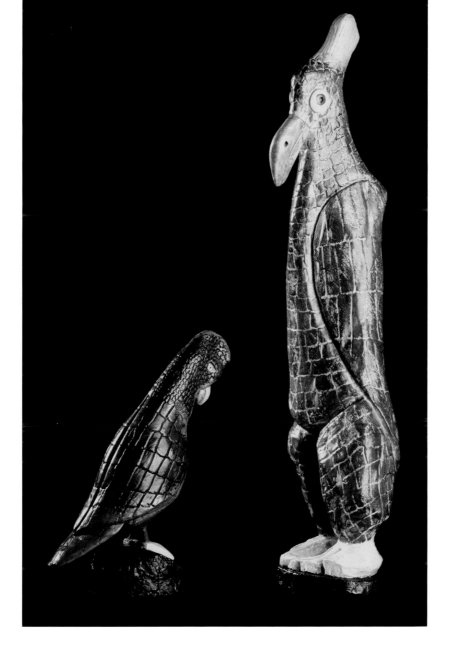

149

Large bird, *1992. Dimensions: 16" h.*
Small bird, *1991. Dimensions: 8" h.*
Acrylic and varnish on cypress.
Artist's Collection.

W.C. RICE

Born February 20, 1930, in Bibb County, Alabama
Lives in Prattville

W. C. Rice got saved on the 24th day of April 1960 at 2 o'clock in the morning. As it turned out, an artist, as well as a Christian, was born. Yet it would be some years before the former would make himself known to the latter.

Rice remembers the whole episode in precise and eerie detail. "I hadn't even went to bed yet," he recalls of that spring night. "I was a-hurtin'. I'd had me an ulcerated stomach all them years, about fifteen years, and it irritated me, and my mind. I knowed there was a God, I believed there was. Don't you? I just asked him if he'd heal me, my ulcerated stomach."

Rice also asked the Lord to save him, and the Lord complied with both requests. The next day, Rice told his wife to put all his stomach medicine in the garbage can. He gave up his only vice, chewing tobacco, and became a devoted Christian on a self-styled mission to convert nonbelievers.

Although he wasn't raised in the church, Rice discovered the joys of salvation with a local Assembly of God congregation and, later, in a Prattville, Alabama, holiness church. He prayed daily. And by 1976, God was talking back.

It was the Lord, Rice says, who instructed him to install three crude wooden four-foot-high crosses in his front yard in Prattville. And it was the Lord, Rice says, who told him to keep up the good work. Rice did, sometimes laboring at it more than eight hours a day.

Before his neighbors could raise much fuss, Rice had covered his front yard and close to three acres of surrounding property with homemade whitewashed crosses of various sizes—from looming crisscrosses of timber that had to be lifted by a backhoe to tiny matchstick-sized crosses dangling from strings in the trees.

On some, Rice—a house painter by trade—dabbled splotches of red, representing the blood of Christ. He emblazoned others with the number 24, commemorating that April morning when he got saved.

Among the hundreds of crosses, Rice erected signs, painted on rotting lumber and junked appliances, bearing Bible verses filled with misspelled words, as well as warnings and instructions for visiting sinners: "Repent." "Hell is hot." "Read the Bible."

With help from his son, Rice built a rickety chapel festooned, of course, with crosses. He set up outdoor tableaus depicting Jesus' birth and death, as well as pits filled with beer cans to represent the ravages of hell. And it was all magnificently defined and outlined by those crude wooden crosses.

Many of Rice's neighbors began to regard him as a religious fanatic who reduced the property value in his rural neighborhood. Yet through the years, he also acquired an appreciative following of students, artists, and the merely curious. They make pilgrimages from around the country to see his incredible cross garden, to talk with him, and sometimes to take a Rice-autographed cross to hang on the wall back home.

Although he enjoys the company, Rice dismisses the notion that he's an artist. "Some people call me an artist. Some people call me a weirdo. I don't care what they call me, you know what I mean? I never been involved in art and that kind of stuff, see. Don't do paintings or nothin' like that. But I get people from all over. They hear about me from other people.

"A guy from California took several pieces to use in an art show. I had a man from Louisiana come down here wanting some of it to put in a museum. He give me seventy-five dollars. That's the most I ever got for any of it."

150

W.C. Rice   6/12/93 Prattville, Alabama

In the beginning, Rice's wife, Marzell, wasn't particularly pleased about all the crosses. She watched them multiply at an alarming rate. She saw them quickly spread into their ranch-style home, where the paneled walls are filled with pictures of Jesus and tiny crosses dangle by the hundreds from the wood-beamed ceiling.

"She's used to it now," Rice says of his wife. "So's most of these other people. It done been here so long it don't bother 'em no more."

Originally from Bibb County, Alabama, near Woodstock, Rice was the oldest of seven children born to truck farmer Carlton Rice and his wife, Annie Mae Hyde. Although Annie Mae was raised in the Baptist Church, she didn't pass her religion down to her children.

"They didn't teach it around me, about being saved, that smokin' and chewin' tobacco and all that stuff was wrong," Rice says. "Before I got saved, I didn't know the difference between God and Jesus and the Holy Ghost, see. I didn't learn nothin' about it."

Rice finished the ninth grade in West Blocton and then dropped out of school to help with the farming. At age 18, he traveled to Florida and found work picking oranges and grapefruit. Two years later, he married Marzell.

They eventually settled in Prattville, where Rice made a living painting houses. He did well enough to support four children, build a brick home, and even open a trailer park behind his house.

Rice had never thought much about crosses until his mother died in the mid-1970s. At her funeral, a wreath of flowers in the shape of a cross caught his eye. He decided a more permanent cross would be a fine way to honor his mother, so he nailed together two pieces of scrap wood and stuck it in the ground at her grave.

Rice's enthusiasm for crosses might have ended there, were it not for the displeasure of the cemetery staff, who said the cross at his mother's grave violated cemetery rules. They removed Rice's cross, and he quickly installed another. Thus began a frenzy of crosses going up and coming down, with the cemetery staff finally threatening legal action. Rice suddenly announced that the Lord had spoken to him, telling him to forget about the cemetery and instead put up three crosses in his front yard.

Rice says his age and bad back now make it impossible for him to keep up the cross garden. Although he periodically sets out a batch of new crosses, he's more likely to be found in his den, watching TV or listening to country music. Outside, the weeds are as high as some of the crosses, now fading and rotting on the hillside by his home.

His neighbors have complained, and preachers have worried that the message of the crosses is one of judgment rather than love. But Rice and his crosses have weathered the storms.

"Some of 'em still think I'm crazy," he says. "It's just like what them people went through in the Bible. People got persecuted 'cause of their religion. That was awful, wasn't it? I ain't gone through something that bad. They ain't chopped my head off yet."

152

Rice often attaches small, painted wood crosses to his larger crosses made from telephone poles.

154

*Many of the crosses on Rice's property are painted with splotches of red
to represent the blood of Christ.*

REVELATIONS

155

*Artists, students, and the merely curious have traveled from around the country
to see Rice's cross garden, located in Prattville, Alabama.*

JUANITA ROGERS

Born May 12, 1934, near Montgomery, Alabama
Died January 26, 1985, in Montgomery

Juanita Rogers called them her "funny brick," the bizarre-looking half-human, half-animal creatures she sculpted out of cow bones and mud in her two-room shack on the outskirts of Montgomery, Alabama.

It was there, in 1981, at the urging of a social worker, that Montgomery artist Anton Haardt first saw Juanita and her brick. Juanita's common-law husband had recently died, leaving her with no means of support. All she owned were those grotesque sculptures, which the social worker hoped Anton Haardt could help Juanita sell.

Ms. Haardt, who eventually became Juanita's friend and mentor, will never forget the day she walked into that shack, which was equipped with a single light bulb and no running water. "The entire house was filled with dirt and dust and mud," Ms. Haardt recalls.

"There was no furniture at all, except a bed and a TV. For her heat and her cooking, Juanita had a big metal drum she would build a fire in, with no chimney, and it had turned the windows black, and smoke would just be going everywhere. She lived a real primitive existence. Not that she had always lived that way, but I didn't know that then."

During the next several years, until Juanita Rogers's death in 1985, Anton Haardt visited often in the dusty shack, where she listened to her friend's strange (and often imagined) tales and observed the personal eccentricities that defined her art.

"She was very suspicious of me at first," Ms. Haardt says. "At the end of that first visit, I wanted to take a small mud piece home with me to show somebody, and Juanita thought I was going to take it to the mental institution to prove that she was crazy and have her committed."

Juanita did, at last, allow Ms. Haardt to borrow a piece of her funny brick, but few people were interested in buying the stuff. And there were other problems with the art. Its bizarre appearance belied its fragile nature. Juanita's mud sculpture, Ms. Haardt discovered, could crumble apart at the slightest touch.

Photo courtesy Anton Haardt.

156

Indian Sun, *ca. 1980.*
Watercolor and pencil on paper. Dimensions: 12" x 12³/₄".
Collection of Anton Haardt.

When she could find no collector or museum to buy Juanita's work, Ms. Haardt began to buy it herself. Juanita initially was reluctant to agree to such an arrangement. She claimed already to have a buyer for her art–a man called "Stonefish," she said, periodically picked up her sculptures and sold them in a store. Juanita claimed Stonefish and her mud sculptures were part of a top-secret FBI investigation.

Anton Haardt eventually concluded that the story of Stonefish, like so many other peculiar tales Juanita told, was the product of a vivid imagination. But while waiting to meet the mysterious (and nonexistent) Stonefish, Ms. Haardt came up with an idea that would allow Juanita to work for her without being disloyal to her make-believe employer.

"I said, 'Well maybe you could work for me making drawings or something,' " Ms. Haardt recalls. She was soon delivering paper, pencils, and paints to the two-room shack, where Juanita's imagination quickly manifested itself in a series of cartoon-like drawings. They were largely inspired by TV characters such as Miss Piggy, Fat Albert, and the Coneheads.

By the time Juanita died, she had produced more than 250 paintings and drawings. Most remain, along with 40 or so of the artist's salvaged mud pieces, in Anton Haardt's private collection.

"We set up an arrangement where I paid to have water pumped into her house and got her the things she needed," Ms. Haardt says. "There was no one really to buy her art. But I knew one day people would. So I took over the responsibility of paying her bills, taking her food, and managing her."

During their four-year association, in talks with Juanita and several members of her family, Ms. Haardt learned bits and pieces of Juanita's life story. Juanita explained that she had been "making mud" since she was five or six years old, which prompted her unappreciative father to reply, "I made mud pies,

too, but that don't mean you have to go losing your mind making mud pies."

Juanita claimed to have been born to a family named Green in a place called "Indian." There, she told Anton Haardt, "the black mud swallows up the cars." She claimed to have caught a carnival train to Montgomery, where, at age five, she was adopted by the Rogers family.

Her father, Thomas Rogers, told a less colorful story, which Ms. Haardt eventually concluded was the truth. Juanita was born and reared in the community of Tintop, near Montgomery, attended Montgomery schools through the ninth grade, and worked for a time as a waitress, dishwasher, and housekeeper.

At age 20, Juanita gave herself an abortion, which resulted in a fibroid tumor that made her appear permanently pregnant. "When the tumor started to grow, she thought it was God punishing her with a baby forever there," says Ms.Haardt. She theorizes that Juanita's interest in burying bones in dirt symbolized her need to bury that baby residing in her stomach.

"She said it was a calcified baby, like a stone, and maybe that's where she got Stonefish," Ms. Haardt says.

Because of the tumor, Juanita kept to herself, becoming more and more reclusive as the years went by. In the 1970s, she settled in the shack with her common-law husband, Sol Huffman. He didn't approve of her funny brick but supported her nonetheless. When he died in 1981, she immersed herself in her art, filling the house with her mud sculptures.

The funny brick was essentially mud with bits of Spanish moss, glass, coffee grounds, and even chimney smut mixed in. Inside each were bones Juanita collected from the cow pastures surrounding her home.

"She told me that once a man from the utility company had come out to her home, and she said to him, 'Come in,

Dog, *ca. 1980.*
Mud, grass, animal bones. Dimensions: 8" h.
Collection of Anton Haardt.

come on in to my house. It's a graveyard in here. I'm just living here, covering bones with dirt,' " Ms. Haardt recalls.

Ms. Haardt suspected that the bones had something to do with voodoo, but Juanita vehemently denied it. "It all looked kind of voodooish because under the bed were all these bones and pigs' teeth in a big box," Ms. Haardt says. "And these monsters she made had a spooky look. They're not pretty. They look like demons. They're scary."

Juanita refused to help Anton Haardt repair and preserve her disintegrating mud pieces. Ms. Haardt eventually found a way, using glue and dowels, to preserve and protect them. She plans to donate them to a museum.

Through Anton Haardt, Juanita came to the attention of museums and collectors. She was the first American woman whose work was exhibited in the Art Brut Museum of Lausanne, Switzerland. When Ms. Haardt began to sell some of Juanita's drawings and paintings, Michael Stipe of the rock group R.E.M. bought a number of pieces, including one used for the cover of the group's 1986 album, "Lifes Rich Pageant."

Even in the last years of her life, Juanita Rogers was a striking woman. With her high cheekbones, rich black complexion, and fragile beauty, she resembled the actress Cicely Tyson. But she wasn't concerned with appearance and rarely bothered to bathe or groom herself.

Her life was her art, and she believed she had an audience. As she told Anton Haardt, her work was for "crippled people, crazy people, and colored people all over the world."

160

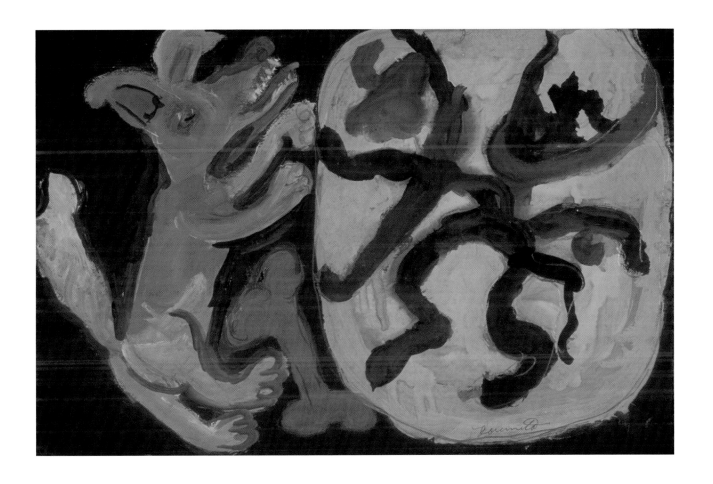

161

Moon Melt, *ca. 1980.*
Watercolor and pencil on paper. Dimensions: 12 1/2" x 19".
Collection of Anton Haardt.

BERNICE SIMS

Born December 25, 1926, in Georgiana, Alabama
Lives in Brewton

Mose Tolliver doesn't know it, but he helped launch Bernice Sims's career as an artist. It happened in the early 1980s, when Mrs. Sims was studying for her associate's degree at Jefferson Davis Community College in Brewton, Alabama. Having long dreamed of a career in art, she was taking an art history course that called for a field trip to the Montgomery Museum of Fine Arts.

"This lady at the museum told us we should go by Mose Tolliver's house before we went back to Brewton," Mrs. Sims recalls. "We went over there, and Mose inspired me so much. He was very famous, and people were going there buying his work and seeing him.

"I looked at his paintings and compared them to mine. I said, 'My goodness, my work, to me, looks better than his.' I said, 'If he can do it, I can too.' And I came home, and that's when I really got started. So I have to give Mose credit."

Since 1984, when she returned from that Montgomery trip with a new inspiration, Bernice Sims has become known for her brightly colored oil and acrylic paintings and the important stories they tell.

Black history, especially the struggle for civil rights, is the focus of much of her work. She has painted the defiant march across the Edmund Pettus Bridge at Selma, as well as the horror of the fire hoses and police dogs in downtown Birmingham.

But she also depicts the daily routine of black southern life, away from the struggle for racial equality. In "Spring Cleaning," she painted a woman beating dust from rugs hanging on a clothesline. Churches are a backdrop in many of her pictures, which show baptisms, weddings, and Sunday school picnics.

"Mostly I'm conveying the history of blacks, the things we're accustomed to," Mrs. Sims says. "I paint the civil rights pictures because I like to keep it alive. There are some things my children and grandchildren and great-grandchildren should know about. And since I can't do any writing, I tell the story in my paintings."

Mrs. Sims played an active role in the civil rights movement during the 1960s. She joined the NAACP and the Alabama Democratic Congress and often attended marches and rallies across Alabama.

She was among the throng of civil rights supporters confronted by the troopers at the bridge in Selma. Then a single mother with six children, she watched the march from the sidelines, afraid of losing her job if she took a more visible role.

Some of her paintings show a gentler relationship between blacks and whites, reflecting her own life in rural Alabama. The oldest of ten children, she was born in Georgiana, to laborer Robert Johnson and his wife, Essie.

When she was a little girl, Bernice moved to the country to live with her grandparents in the community of Hickory Hill, where blacks and whites were neighbors and friends. Next door to her grandparents lived a white household of four spinster sisters and their unmarried brother. One of the sisters was an artist, who offered informal training to young Bernice.

"I practically lived at her house," Mrs. Sims recalls. "She'd show me how to do little things. I always wanted to paint but couldn't afford it. I didn't have anything to do it with. So I'd do my drawings with crayon on paper. I drew anything that came into my mind—dogs, people, houses. I loved to draw houses."

Bernice dropped out of the ninth grade to marry a laborer named Willie James Sims. In 1945, not long after

Bernice Sims   7/11/93 Brewton, Alabama

they wed, the couple moved south to Brewton to be closer to his family.

There, Mrs. Sims settled into her role as wife and mother, giving birth to six children. But her marriage didn't last. By the time her oldest child was in high school, Mrs. Sims was a young divorcee raising her children alone.

She supported them by washing and ironing clothes in private homes. But she never stopped dreaming of a better day. In the late 1970s, when her children were grown and beginning lives of their own, Mrs. Sims went back to school and emerged with her GED certificate.

Several years later, she signed up for classes at the community college, where her interest in art was rekindled. After earning an associate's degree in 1984, she began to concentrate on painting.

At first, she painted on wood, masonite, and a variety of other surfaces, as Mose Tolliver had been doing for years. But Mrs. Sims came to prefer working on canvas with acrylic and oil paint. Although she has a small art studio behind her house, she has been working in her bedroom lately, away from the flu-inducing drafts of the studio.

In recent years, she has suffered from severe arthritis and other health problems. But Mrs. Sims vows to keep on painting "as long as I'm able to use my hands, and see, and think, and get the inspiration to do it."

Adam and Eve, *1992.*
Oil on composite board. Dimensions: 15 1/4" x 30 1/4".
Robert Cargo Folk Art Gallery, Tuscaloosa, Alabama.

BERNICE SIMS

166

Birmingham Waterhose, *1993.*
Acrylic on canvas. Dimensions: 22" x 28".
Artist's Collection.

Tent Revival, *1993.*
Acrylic on canvas. Dimensions: 20" x 16".
Artist's Collection.

JEWELL STARDAY

**Born September 11, 1938, in Bessemer, Alabama
Lives in Birmingham**

Until August 1993, Jewell Starday thought life had passed her by.

Born Bettie Jean Brown, she had grown up poor in New York City, dropped out of high school, endured a miserable marriage, seen five of her twelve children die from accidents or sickness, and generally been unhappy for most of her 55 years.

In the mid-1980s, her children were beginning lives of their own. So she went back to school, got her high school equivalency certificate, and enrolled in the College of New Rochelle, New York, where in 1991 she received a degree in social science.

She dreamed of working as a counselor after first traveling the world as a Peace Corps volunteer. She'd gone so far as to send away for the brochures when reality smacked her in the face. Her son, Lonnie, was graduating from law school and needed her to help him establish his practice. And her youngest child, Hope, needed a place to come home to between semesters at Alabama State University.

So Bettie Jean settled into a two-bedroom apartment in a run-down neighborhood in Birmingham, Alabama. Once again she spent her days tending to the needs of others. She answered the phone in Lonnie's small law office, where, in August 1993, she found herself doodling with a pen on the back of his message pad.

In a few days, she had accumulated a stack of doodles and carried them home to show her daughter. Hope was impressed enough to buy her mother a supply of acrylic and watercolor paints, which Bettie Jean used to give color to her drawings.

By New Year's Day 1994, just four months after she began doodling, Bettie Jean had completed nearly 500 paintings—enough to cover the walls of her apartment from floor to ceiling. And suddenly, she felt wonderful.

"It was like I had to paint these pretty pictures to erase the ugly ones inside me," she explains, standing in her living room, surrounded by art. "I look at these pictures, and I feel good."

Among her paintings, done mostly on white office paper or corrugated cardboard, are the glittery, fluorescent images of African kings and queens. Others are simpler pictures of people and animals. And some are nothing more than swirling circles of color representing, to her, the idea of karma, or "what goes around comes around," which also sums up her philosophy of life.

A predominant image in her pictures is a single, dark-skinned woman—initially pictured sad and mousy, but more recently shown as a goddess, descending from the heavens. "I call her Jewell Starday," the artist says.

Jewell Starday is also what Bettie Jean now calls herself. She signs that name on her paintings and recently made it her legal identity. "There's a lot in a name. I never liked Bettie Jean. I had to find something I thought was me. Jewels have everlasting light in them, don't they? The daystar is the sun, and what's that? Everlasting light.

"I chose that name because it has meaning to me. It makes me feel good. Bettie Jean maybe made somebody else feel good, but I never liked it."

Bettie Jean Brown was born in Bessemer, Alabama, and raised by her grandparents until she was old enough to go to school. At age six, she went to live with her mother and stepfather, a coal miner who worked hard to provide for a family of twelve children.

Jewell Starday   12/30/93 Birmingham, Alabama

When the mines closed down, the family moved to Brooklyn, New York, where Bettie Jean's stepfather shined shoes and worked in factories. After completing the eleventh grade, Bettie Jean quit school, got married, and gave birth in 1956 to the first of her 12 babies.

Her husband, she says, failed in his role as provider, leaving her and her children penniless for months at a time. To make ends meet, Bettie would knock on doors in the Jewish neighborhoods, where she found day work as a housekeeper. During the worst of times, she and eight of her children shared a one-room attic apartment.

Lacking money for good medical care, she watched several of her babies die in infancy from pneumonia and other maladies. Even worse was the mysterious death of her oldest son, Charles, who police said was electrocuted when he fell onto subway tracks.

Miserable as she was, Bettie Jean managed to keep going, if only because of her children. "They really needed me," she says. "And I didn't want those little people to grow up feeling like I felt. So I had to do everything I could to make them feel good about themselves."

In 1978, when her sons were old enough to be impressed by the street-corner hoodlums in New York, Bettie Jean decided it was time to move. She packed up her children and returned to her native Alabama, convinced the slower pace was more suited to raising teenage boys.

About that time, she started writing poems. At first they were simple rhymes about her children, but later Bettie Jean composed verses exploring a spirituality more complex than what she had learned as a child.

"I was brought up Baptist down here in Alabama. In New York, we got with the holiness church. I wouldn't say that turned me off to religion, but it was like a launching pad for something better."

As her children grew older and began to start families, Bettie Jean went back to New York and enrolled in college, thinking she still had time to fulfill a long-felt need. Travel and excitement were what she thought would make her happy.

Degree in hand, she returned to Alabama in 1992, planning to stay "just a while," until her son got his law practice established. But by August 1993, almost a year had passed, and she began to feel "stressed out."

Her doodles and paintings were like therapy, giving her an energy and calling she never thought possible. "Some days I paint twenty-five pictures," she says. "It makes me feel so good, I just don't want to stop. It seems like a miracle. It's just amazing to me."

The Guiding Light, *1993.*
Acrylic, ink on cardboard. Dimensions: 16" x 20".
Private Collection.

172

Self-portrait, *1993.*
Acrylic, ink on paper. Dimensions: 8 ½ " x 11".
Private Collection.

Racquel and Jonathan, *1993.*
Acrylic, ink on paper. Dimensions: 22" x 28".
Artist's Collection.

JIMMY LEE SUDDUTH

Born March 10, 1910, in Fayette County, Alabama
Lives in Fayette

"Whoo-wee! Let me think," Jimmy Lee Sudduth says when a visitor asks how many years he's been an artist. He glances at the ceiling in his small frame house and then scratches himself on the chin.

"I started drawin' when I was three years old, and I been drawin' ever since," he finally says. "I always used mud. That's right. And charcoal out of the fireplace. My mama was a medicine doctor, you know. She'd go out and get stuff outdoors, and I'd be drawing on a tree with the charcoal and mud."

Sudduth laughs loudly and shakes his head at the recollection. He never dreamed that one day his charcoal and mud pictures would be sought after by collectors around the world and even displayed prominently in his hometown, at the Fayette Art Museum.

"I got people coming to see me from New York and Chicago and California–that's the end of the world, as far as you can go," he says. "People come see me, and they tell other people, and now just everybody comes."

At age 84, Sudduth isn't able to entertain all the visitors in the style he would like. In years gone by, before his heart problems began to sap his energy and enthusiasm, he not only welcomed uninvited strangers into his home, but he also entertained them with his harmonica playing.

His poor health also has slowed down his painting. Yet he's still producing a surprising quantity of his unique mud pictures depicting life in rural Fayette County. He draws on scrap plywood, using pencil, charcoal, or bits of gravel he finds in the street in front of his house. Then he dips his finger into a bucket of his special mud mixture, which he rubs onto his pictures to give them color and texture.

He taught himself the technique as a small boy, not long after he drew his first picture on a tree. "It was an old-time log house I seen when I was three years old," he recalls of his first drawing. "The rain come and washed the mud and charcoal off the tree. How I got it to stay there, I went up to Dave Musgrove's place, he was a big syrup maker, and he threw some of that syrup on the ground, and it splashed up and went on the tree, and I couldn't get it off. And I told him, 'I got what I want now.'"

Jimmy Lee began coating his drawings with syrup, which preserved them better than even shellac. Later, when he didn't have enough syrup, he began mixing sugar water in with his mud, which worked almost as well as the syrup.

Born and reared in the community of Caines Ridge near Fayette, Jimmy Lee didn't get much schooling–barely enough, he says, to write his name. He lived with his stepfather and mother, who made medicinal potions from plants and weeds growing near her home. Years later, Sudduth would often rub those same weeds and berries, as well as petals from roses and other flowers, across his drawings to add bright splashes of color to the mud.

As he grew up, Jimmy Lee set aside his art to work as a farm laborer. He married young and had one daughter. After his first wife died, Sudduth married Ethel Palmore and remained devoted to her for more than 50 years, until her death in 1992.

In the 1950s, Jimmy Lee and Ethel left their country community and moved closer to town, where Sudduth became a popular gardener. By the late 1960s, he was slowing down his yard work and devoting more and more time to his mud paintings.

Jimmy Lee Sudduth   7/17/93 Fayette, Alabama

JIMMY LEE SUDDUTH

Among the gardener's clients was Jack Black, director of the Fayette Art Museum. Black had no idea his friend Jimmy Lee was an artist until Sudduth knocked on his door in 1970 and showed him one of his mud paintings.

Astounded by Jimmy Lee's creativity and imagination, both in subject matter and artistic method, Black eventually put together a show of Sudduth's work at the Fayette museum.

If the townspeople were surprised to see their favorite gardener in a one-man exhibition, Sudduth was downright astonished. He had assumed his city friends wouldn't be interested in his mud pictures "because it's dirt, but it turns out that's what they wanted. Now I'm hangin' in all the museums, all over the place. I'm in folks' houses all over town."

Log houses, like the one he drew as a boy, have been the subjects of many of Sudduth's paintings. Among his favorite subjects, too, are old churches and public buildings, as well as Indian women, farm animals, and plowmen with their mules. He has painted innumerable pictures of Toto, the name he gives to almost all his dogs.

Jimmy Lee traveled to Washington, D.C., in 1976 as one of two Alabama artists invited to the Smithsonian Institution's bicentennial Festival of American Folklife. Art lovers there not only got to enjoy his paintings, but also got to hear Jimmy Lee play his harmonica.

Two years later, the Birmingham Museum of Art mounted an exhibit of Sudduth's work. And in 1980, the artist was featured in a segment on the network television program "Today." His paintings can be found in galleries across the country.

"I been to Canada, up there at Niagara Falls. I been to Washington. I went up there and the people just went crazy for me. They wanted to know what I was runnin' for, up there in Washington," he says.

Sudduth's visits north inspired his work throughout the 1980s. He created a mud painting of the United States Capitol and another of the New York City skyline. In recent years, he has increasingly used house paint to give color to his pictures, although just about all contain at least a small amount of mud.

"That won't come off, it's guaranteed," the artist says as he applies mud to yet another log cabin. "It's gonna stay there. You can't kick it off or wash it off, I guarantee it."

When his mud buckets are near empty, Sudduth gets a friend or relative to take him into the country, where he can replenish his supply. He claims that the dirt in Alabama alone comes in 36 colors–from blue and red to black and white. And he knows where to find every shade.

Sudduth's success as an artist has earned him "more money than you ever seen" and more friends than he can keep track of. If he's feeling up to it, he pulls out his instant camera and snaps his visitors' pictures, which he keeps in an old shoebox under his bed.

"I know all these people," he says, dumping the contents of the box onto his bed. "Every one of 'em been to my house. Some of 'em call me up and talk my ear off. Somebody's always wantin' a painting."

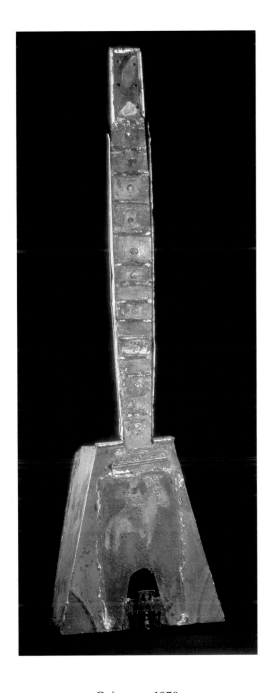

Guitar, *ca. 1970.*
Wood, curtain rods, buttons, mud, paint. Dimensions: 48" h.
Collection of Georgine and Jack Clarke.

178

Indian Girl, ca. 1960.
Mud and house paint on wood. Dimensions: 10" x 8".
Robert Cargo Folk Art Gallery, Tuscaloosa, Alabama.

Toto, *1985.*
Mud and house paint on plywood. Dimensions: 24" x 12".
Robert Cargo Folk Art Gallery, Tuscaloosa, Alabama.

Statue of Liberty, *n.d.*
Mud, house paint, chewing gum on board.
Dimensions: 37" x 11 ½".
Robert Cargo Folk Art Gallery, Tuscaloosa, Alabama.

Tokyo Pepsi Cola, *1987.*
Mud, house paint, caulking compound, Pepsi cans on plywood.
Dimensions: 27 1/2" x 27 1/2".
Robert Cargo Folk Art Gallery, Tuscaloosa, Alabama.

181

Church, *1976.*
Mud and paint on board. Dimensions: 24" x 36".
Collection of Kurt Gitter and Alice Yelen.

MOSE TOLLIVER

Born July 4, about 1920, in Montgomery County, Alabama
Lives in Montgomery

Strangers roam through Mose Tolliver's two-story Sayre Street house in Montgomery, Alabama, as if it were a museum, free and open to the public. They come at all hours, every day of the week, often to buy paintings, and just as often merely to visit with the artist.

From his seat in the middle of his unmade bed, the white-haired Tolliver watches them come and go, answers their questions and occasionally tries to hawk one of his paintings, which decorate nearly every wall.

"That's fifty dollars," he tells a well-dressed man examining one of the vibrant watermelon pictures hanging over the bed. A paint-splattered radio plays gospel music as Tolliver, dressed in a tee-shirt and dark pants, begins another painting on the makeshift easel in his lap.

Frequent visitors know that Tolliver's prices vary, depending on how he's feeling, and if he likes you, and whether he's been enjoying some of the homemade whiskey that occasionally comes his way.

When he's feeling well, as he seems to be on this summer morning, he happily talks about his life and his art, though never without a certain degree of matter-of-factness.

"I ain't interested in no art," he says, repeating a claim he has made for years. "I just like to do my pictures."

He most often works with house paint on pieces of plywood, although chairs, suitcases, tabletops, trays, and a variety of other unlikely surfaces brought to him by friends and fans frequently accommodate his brush.

His earliest paintings, done in the late 1960s, were of birds. But he soon expanded his repertoire to include a variety of animals, especially snakes, and people, among them George Washington, Martin Luther King, Jr., Jesus Christ, and Mose

Tolliver himself. He completes many pictures by painting a black stripe around the border. Often, he attaches a beer can pop-top to the back of a painting to hang it on the wall.

Among his most popular images are his "moose ladies" and "ladies on scooters," which depict smiling, spread-legged women straddling giant phalluses detailed to resemble bicycles.

Those, and many of his paintings, display a sly sense of humor. Others depict creatures that are frighteningly beastlike. He signs his work "Mose T," with a backward S, among the most recognizable monikers in modern folk art.

Tolliver's stories of his life vary as much as the prices on his pictures, though a significant portion of his tale usually stays the same: In the late 1960s, when he was working in the shipping department of a furniture company, a box of marble fell on his legs, crippling him and forcing him to quit work.

His boss at the furniture company, a man who painted for a hobby, encouraged him to take painting lessons. Mose declined, opting to teach himself. The first thing he painted was a red bird, done with house paint on old pasteboard. A woman paid him three dollars for it, launching Tolliver's career.

"After that, I painted birds for two or three years 'cause I didn't know nothin' else to paint," he says. By the mid-1970s, he was painting whatever popped into his mind, displaying it in front of his house.

Among early fans who helped bring his work to the public were Montgomery artist Anton Haardt and Mitchell Kahan, former curator of the Montgomery Museum of Fine Arts. In 1981, the museum mounted a one-man show of Tolliver's work. The next year, his paintings were included in the major national exhibition "Black Folk Art in America, 1930-1980," mounted by the prestigious Corcoran Gallery of Art in Washington, D.C.

182

Mose Tolliver   6/28/93 montgomery, Alabama

By the mid-1980s, Tolliver had such a huge following that even his ten-paintings-a-day output couldn't handle the demand. So in 1985, he hired his daughter Annie Tolliver to help him paint his pictures. She would duplicate his images and colors, and he would add the finishing touch with his distinctive "Mose T" signature.

"That went on for about four years," says Annie, who went on her own as a painter in 1989 and has become almost as popular an artist as her father.

She recalls the early days in Mose's painting career, when none of his family members seemed to appreciate or understand what he was doing. "I didn't like it, I know that," Annie says, sitting on the front porch of her house, just a few blocks from her father's home.

"He was doing moose ladies, animals, dogs, same as he's doing now. I didn't understand what it was 'til he told me, and then I got interested and liked it. The moose lady, with her legs all up in the air, I really didn't understand what it was. He told me it was a lady that, whenever she gets ready for a man, she goes out and uses her exercise bike, and then she don't need no man. That's one of his favorites."

Mose Tolliver was born on a farm near Montgomery, where his father was a sharecropper and his mother struggled to raise a houseful of children. Like his brothers and sisters, Mose worked the fields and attended school sparingly. He dropped out altogether after finishing the third grade.

As a young man, he hauled and sold vegetables, worked as a gardener, and painted houses, often finishing the doors and windows with artistic flourishes that weren't necessarily appreciated by his customers.

In the 1940s, he married Willie Mae Thomas. The couple had 13 children. After Mose started painting, Willie Mae didn't always enjoy the uninvited guests who dropped in to buy art or meet the artist. And she didn't approve of Mose's moose ladies hanging in her house.

After Willie Mae died in 1991, Mose had greater opportunity to indulge in his fondness for drinking, which, as Annie recalls, sometimes caused problems when she was growing up. "He was a good father when he was sober and the devil when he was drunk," she says.

Yet it was a kindhearted Mose who encouraged Annie to pursue her art, telling her, "You can't hurt me. Keep up the good work." And he hasn't minded the more recent competition from two of his sons, Annie's younger brothers Charlie and Jimmy, who began painting in the early 1990s.

Mose says he likes to have visitors at his home, which he shares with several of his children. His art enabled him to pay for his house as well as a parcel of Montgomery property he hopes will one day be valuable.

He's never had an art lesson and even turned down an offer by his old boss at the furniture company to pay his way through art school. "I said I'd rather learn myself," Tolliver recalls. "He said, 'How you know you'll do it right?' I said, 'If somebody buys it, then it's right.'"

Willie Mae, *ca. 1969.*
House paint on cardboard. Dimensions: 15" x 9½".
Collection of Anton Haardt.

186

Vodka Birds, ca. 1973-74.
House paint on tabletop, painted on both sides. Dimensions: 23" x 20 3/4".
Collection of Marcia and Kim Weber.

Tricycle Lady, *1987.*
Paint on plywood. Dimensions: 22" x 19".
Collection of Diane Derzis.

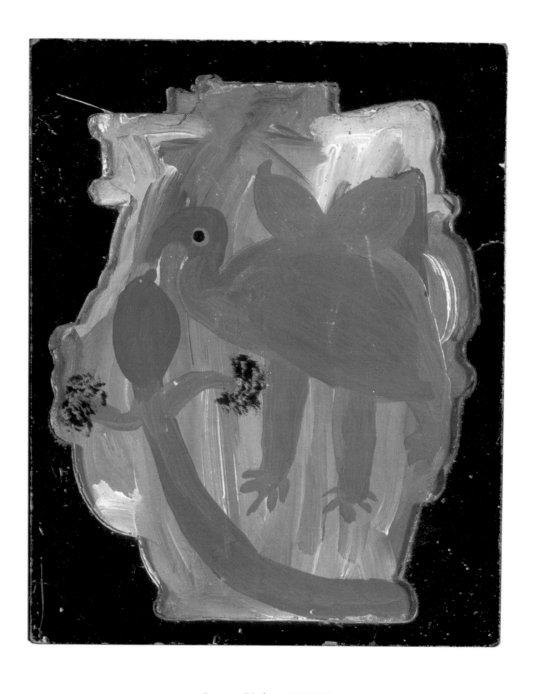

Orange Bird, *ca. 1974-75.*
House paint on jigsaw puzzle. Dimensions: 11 ½" x 9 ½".
Collection of Marcia and Kim Weber.

Self-portrait, *1987.*
Paint and hair on plywood. Dimensions: 27" x 18".
Collection of Diane Derzis.

190

Bus, *1987.*
House paint on plywood. Dimensions: 14" x 17".
Collection of Diane Derzis.

Annie Tolliver, Crucifixion (signed by Mose T), 1987.
House paint on plywood. Dimensions: 21" x 14".
Robert Cargo Folk Art Gallery, Tuscaloosa, Alabama.

BILL TRAYLOR

**Born about 1854 near Benton, Alabama
Died 1947 in Montgomery**

Bill Traylor could neither read nor write, and he wasn't inclined to waste his breath in casual conversation, recalls his 70-year-old granddaughter, Margaret Elizabeth Traylor Staffney of Montgomery, Alabama. "He was quiet. If you wanted to know anything, you had to ask him," Mrs. Staffney says.

Yet Traylor managed to speak volumes through his drawings and paintings, which he began producing on the streets of Montgomery in the late 1930s, when he was 85 years old.

Mrs. Staffney can still see him sitting there, in a doorway on Monroe Street, using a pencil stub and a straightedge to create images of people and animals on beat-up cardboard. He drew what he had seen and lived in rural Benton, Alabama, where he was born into slavery a decade before the War Between the States and remained in emancipation for 70 years.

A man plowing with a mule, a woman milking a cow, a dog nursing her pups, a pair of mad dogs tangling in battle–these were among the simple stories Traylor told through his art.

His granddaughter, who stopped by to say hello whenever she was on Monroe Street, remembers seeing him bent down in concentration over his work, his black forehead glistening with sweat. "He'd be drawing horses, dogs, pigs, cows, ladies, and men," she recalls. "And I'd make fun of 'em. I'd say, 'You can't do nothin' with this.' "

During their visits, Mrs. Staffney would ask questions of the gray-bearded, heavyset Traylor, who would sometimes begin crying in the midst of their conversation. She believes his tears, as well as his art, were prompted by bad memories from long ago.

"He'd be talking, and all of a sudden, he'd start crying. You never really knew what triggered it. Maybe he was remember-ing when he was a slave. Once, he told me about how he hid in a tree stump during the fighting, after the Yankees came.

"All those memories is what made him draw. It's like when you've been incarcerated, you have to do something to occupy your mind. And he'd do this to forget about his past."

Traylor–who took his name from his plantation master, George Traylor–was 11 years old when the slaves were freed at

Photo courtesy Robert Cargo Folk Art Gallery.

192

Construction with Figures and Animals, *ca. 1939.*
Pencil and poster paint on cardboard. Dimensions: 12" x 8".
Private Collection.

the end of the war. But he chose to stay on at the plantation, where he worked as a field hand, married, and fathered a number of children.

In the late 1930s, after his wife had died, his children had moved away, and most of the white people he knew from the plantation were long gone, Traylor moved to Montgomery. There, he worked for a time in a shoe factory, until rheumatism forced him to go on federal relief.

It was then, with nothing else to keep him busy, that he started drawing his stark and striking geometrical figures, using whatever materials he could scrounge on the streets of downtown Montgomery.

Although he had children and grandchildren scattered around the country, he had no real home and seemed to prefer it that way. At night, Traylor would unroll his pallet in the back room of the Ross-Clayton Funeral Home, where he slept surrounded by caskets. He ate most of his meals and used the bathroom in a nearby cafe.

Traylor used strings to hang his work on a fence near his sidewalk drawing post. People soon began to notice his pictures, and some even bought them for nickels and dimes, which, as his granddaughter recalls, Traylor kept in a tobacco sack by his feet.

Among those who took an interest in Traylor was a 24-year-old Montgomery artist named Charles Shannon, who became his best friend and steadfast promoter. Shannon brought Traylor pencils, poster paints, and other art supplies and even arranged a show of his work in 1940 at Montgomery's New South Art Center.

Shannon, who still lives in Montgomery, declines most interviews these days. In a letter dated December 12, 1993, he states, "As time has gone on, Bill Traylor's fame has continued to grow and my role as a provider of information about him has become more than I can handle."

Until he was drafted in 1942 to serve during World War II, Shannon visited Traylor regularly and began collecting his work. During Shannon's tour with the army, Traylor left Montgomery for a time to live with various children in Detroit and Washington, D.C.

In 1946, when Shannon returned to Montgomery after the war, he found Traylor sitting by a downtown fruit stand with a drawing board in his lap. By then, Traylor had lost one leg to gangrene and was in failing health. Not long afterward, he reluctantly went to live with a daughter in Montgomery and later moved into a nursing home, where he died in 1947.

Shannon was left with the bulk of the 1,500 or so paintings and drawings Traylor produced from 1939 to 1942. After storing the work for 25 years, Shannon retrieved it in the mid-1970s and set about cleaning and cataloging it, hoping to bring it to the public's attention.

In 1979, when folk art was becoming increasingly popular, a new gallery in New York briefly presented Traylor's work in a one-man show. But Traylor's importance in the art world wasn't established until 1982, when his work was featured in the Corcoran Gallery of Art's landmark touring exhibition "Black Folk Art in America, 1930-1980."

Margaret Staffney, whose father, Willie Traylor, was Bill Traylor's son, says family members were astounded to learn that their long-deceased relative's work had become so valuable.

Those family members who noticed his drawings all those years ago seemed, at the time, to share her opinion: that Bill Traylor was a sweet, sad, and lonely old man just trying to stay busy.

Owl, *ca. 1939.*
Poster paint on cardboard. Dimensions: 11" x 8".
Private Collection.

196

Dog, *ca. 1939-42.*
Colored pencil on cardboard. Dimensions: 8" x 9 3/4".
Collection of Kurt Gitter and Alice Yelen.

Man and Woman, *ca. 1940.*
Tempera and pencil on cardboard. Dimensions: 15" x 12 ½".
Private Collection.

198

Man, *ca. 1939.*
Pencil on cardboard. Dimensions: 13 1/4" x 7 1/4".
Private Collection.

Construction with Figures and Animals, *ca. 1940.*
Tempera and pencil on cardboard. Dimensions: 12 ½" x 7".
Private Collection.

FRED WEBSTER

Born February 10, 1911, in Fayette County, Alabama
Lives in Berry

Fred Webster reaches deep into his right trousers pocket and pulls out what looks like a beat-up Boy Scout knife. He opens it and gingerly fingers the blade.

"Right there is the best knife I've ever had," he says in his soft country drawl. "Look how much it's worn out. I can whet that on a stone, and then get down and carve with it. I think it cost a dollar, and it's still my main knife."

That dollar knife, in Webster's big hands, turns ordinary basswood into whimsical figurines that depict Biblical scenes, such as Adam and Eve in the Garden of Eden, and the woodcarver's secular heroes, including former Alabama governor George Wallace and deceased University of Alabama football coach Paul "Bear" Bryant.

Although his work can be found in galleries and collections across the country, Webster still charges his "customers" the nominal sums he earned for his work in the mid-1970s, when he was just beginning his woodcarving hobby. "If you come see me and don't buy anything, I'll be just as satisfied," he rarely neglects to tell a visitor.

When his guests inform him that galleries are asking hundreds of dollars for carvings he sells for less than $50, Webster says he doesn't mind. "Those gallery people run the risk of having to keep it a long time," he explains. "And as far as I'm concerned, it's not altogether about money."

Webster first tried woodcarving after retiring in 1973 from his job as principal at Berry High School in Fayette County, Alabama. Looking for a hobby, he took ceramics classes and then painting lessons at a local junior college. He found neither particularly fulfilling.

In 1975, when his wife retired from her teaching job, the two traveled to the John C. Campbell Folk School in Brasstown, North Carolina, where they spent two weeks learning the craft of the mountain people. Mrs. Webster studied weaving while her husband tried woodcarving.

Back home, as his wife knitted afghans by the woodburning stove in their den, he sat across from her, carving wooden bowls and little animals, especially deer and unicorns. In those days, he used scrap pieces of cedar, white pine, and other wood he often got free at area furniture factories.

Proud of his work, Webster soon began carting it to nearby Northport to show in the annual Kentuck Festival of the Arts. There, in the mid-1980s, a folk art collector and dealer named Robert Cargo introduced himself to Webster and complimented him on his carvings.

Cargo asked Webster if he would carve him a piece depicting the Last Supper. It turned out so well that Webster was soon carving his interpretation of the stories of Jonah and the whale, the birth of Jesus, the Crucifixion, and Noah and the Ark. He created choirs of angels and devils, as well as gatherings of religious snake-handlers.

A finished Biblical scene often included a dozen or more separate carvings, which Webster coated with colorful acrylic paint and then mounted on a plywood base. Many of his ideas, he says, came from visitors who made their way to his home in the late 1980s.

In more recent years, Webster has had to put aside his hobby to take care of his ailing wife, Nell, who has Alzheimer's disease. In the spring of 1993, he finally had to put her in a nursing home, where he visits her daily for hours, even though she no longer seems to know him.

"I go to the nursing home about 12:30 every day, and I'm pretty well there all afternoon," he says. "I talk to her,

Fred Webster   7/30/93 Berry, Alabama

but she doesn't even remember me. There are times she'll grin a little."

Webster's brick home, across the street from Berry High School, is still decorated with his wife's handmade afghans and doilies. The den, where they used to sit close while working on their hobbies, is littered with the wood shavings of Webster's most recent work.

Webster first tinkered with woodcarving as a child growing up in rural Fayette County, near the small town of Winfield. His father was a farmer and his mother a homemaker who took care of their five children.

Although young Fred, like the other Webster children, helped with the farm chores, his ambition was to become a teacher. He left home to attend the Florence State Teachers College (now the University of North Alabama) and graduated in 1940.

By the time he earned his master's degree at the University of Alabama, he was already well into his career as a history and science teacher. After spending two decades as a teacher at two Fayette County junior high schools, he moved to Berry High School as principal and part-time teacher in 1956.

He and Nell, who also worked at Berry High, had three children. One of them is now a counselor at the school.

Through the years, Webster says, he did a little woodcarving in his spare time. "I didn't really stay at it. I was just dribbling around, doing little odd things. But I always enjoyed it." After he retired and became involved in his hobby, Webster often worked eight hours or more a day on his Biblical woodcarvings. Before his wife's illness, Webster regularly indulged himself in another passion–travel. He's been to Israel, Russia, Brazil, and Australia. "I've been to every continent of the world, believe it or not," he says. "It's just in me to travel. If you want to go to the most beautiful place in the world, go to New Zealand. They got the friendliest people in the world, too."

His travels occasionally inspired his carvings. After a trip to Russia in the 1980s, he made his own version of the famous nesting dolls. In Mexico, he bought several primitive wooden toys and brought them home to see if he could duplicate them.

Webster's big hands don't do much carving these days, though the orders for his work continue to come in. "I still get a lot of people calling me up," says Webster, whose hearing problems make it difficult for him to talk on the phone. "People know about me, from traveling around and seeing my work."

Every now and then, in the evenings after a visit with his wife, Webster will pull out that well-worn dollar knife and go to work by the wood-burning stove, across from his wife's empty chair. "Sometimes I get a little lonesome," he says. "This helps me pass the time."

Adam Please Take This Fruit, ca. 1985.
Acrylic on wood. Dimensions: 12" h.
Robert Cargo Folk Art Gallery, Tuscaloosa, Alabama.

FRED WEBSTER

204

Jonah and the Whale, *1986.*
Acrylic on wood. Dimensions: 4 3/4" h.
Collection of Robley M. Hood.

Sweet Drams (sic) Boaz,
Christ is Guarding You, *ca. 1985.*
Acrylic on wood. Dimensions: 18" h.
Robert Cargo Folk Art Gallery, Tuscaloosa, Alabama.

The Crucifixion, *1987.*
Acrylic and fabric on wood. Dimensions: 11 1/2" h.
Collection of Robley M. Hood.

YVONNE WELLS

**Born December 26 in Tuscaloosa, Alabama
Lives in Tuscaloosa**

Sitting in the living room of her spacious brick home in Tuscaloosa, Alabama, Yvonne Wells appears both fit and fashionable.

She is dressed in black walking shoes and a satiny black jogging suit with leopard-print trim. It is the attire of the well-dressed physical education teacher, which is what Mrs. Wells has been for more than 25 years.

She knows it may seem curious that an active, outdoorsy woman would take up a sedentary, indoor hobby such as quilting. But it's like therapy, she says. It brings her a comfort and satisfaction she hadn't thought possible outside the realm of athletics. "Quilting is soothing," she says. "It gives me a very healing feeling. It has a certain spirituality to it."

She has been a quilter for about 15 years, and a storytelling quilter for about a decade. Her first quilt, made in 1979, was designed to keep her warm, but the act of creating also gave her such enjoyment she was determined to do more.

Her early quilts were simple patchwork coverlets, often variations on traditional patterns. Sewn by hand, they were distinctly imperfect. And that gave them character and uniqueness in the eyes of the quilter, never one to make things by the book.

"I can't draw, I don't write well, but I was always good at fixing things," she says. "And I'd always try to make whatever it was a little different, I guess to compensate for it not being exactly right."

Her quilts are indeed distinct, with their uneven sides, erratic stitching, and surprising decorations, such as zippers, buttons, and even fishing line. If something doesn't fit right, she improvises.

"I don't really have the discipline to sit there and make two seams fit," she says. "I've tried to make clothes for my children, but I just couldn't make it work. I don't have the discipline to make things look the way people think they ought to. And that's where the art came in, to make the thing work."

Mrs. Wells has made dozens of story quilts in what she's come to identify as four categories: sociopolitical; religious; children's; and potluck, or whatever strikes her fancy with the leftovers from projects in the first three categories.

Among those in the first category are her tribute to Martin Luther King, Jr., and her portrayals of the struggles for civil rights. For children, she depicts Mickey Mouse or nursery rhymes, such as the story of Humpty Dumpty.

Her strong religious beliefs inspired one of her first story quilts—a simple depiction of the Crucifixion, with Jesus and the two thieves rendered almost as stick figures. Another early Biblical quilt, "Moses on the Mountain," features similarly simplistic stick people below a more realistically rendered Moses holding, toward the sun, the tablets containing the Ten Commandments.

"I've never talked very much, simply because I was always doing something," Mrs. Wells says. "So I put it in the quilts. That lets me say what I feel. Because a lot of times I am without words."

She began doing the story quilts around 1983 because she felt she needed a new direction in her hobby. "I think I had come to the end of the patchwork quilt, as far as I could see it. It wasn't rewarding like it was in prior years.

"I'm a person who needs change," says Mrs. Wells, whose quilts were featured in the groundbreaking exhibition "Stitching Memories: African-American Story Quilts," organized in 1989 by the Williams College Museum of Art in Williamstown, Massachusetts. "That's what keeps you alive. In

Yvonne Wells   11/19/93 Tuscaloosa, Alabama

YVONNE WELLS

staying alive, I see new directions. I just thought I could tell a story on a quilt."

Although she never had any training in art or sewing, Yvonne sometimes watched her mother make utilitarian quilts. "They were quilts you'd make today and use tonight," she recalls.

She grew up in a family of nine children a few blocks from her current home, in the shadow of historic Stillman College. Her mother was an elementary schoolteacher and her father a Presbyterian minister who died when Yvonne was a girl.

Even then, she loved the outdoors. "I loved doing yard work, cutting firewood, and doing anything that was not supposed to be feminine. I just could not stand housework. And to this day I can't. I'm so untidy, not organized at all. And I guess my artwork reflects that."

But she didn't spend her girlhood thinking about art. She was a standout athlete, especially in tumbling and track, and she dreamed about college athletic scholarships and even making the United States Olympic team.

As Yvonne was just beginning to look for a good track and field school to begin her college education, her mother was diagnosed with cancer. So like every one of her siblings, she enrolled in Stillman College. Close to home, she could look after her ailing mother, who died before Yvonne graduated.

"I don't know how promising my track career was, but it was my intention to go all the way, as far as I could," she says. "I don't regret it. The regrets would come in if I hadn't gone to college at all."

Instead of becoming a world-class athlete, she earned a degree in physical education, married a fellow Stillman graduate, and had two children, settling into a comfortable life as a working mother. Her husband, Livingston, was a marine who spent his career in the military.

After he retired, Livingston Wells decided to add a family room with a fireplace to the back of their home. It was there, in 1979, that Yvonne made her first patchwork quilt after finding the fire didn't keep her legs warm enough.

And 15 years later, she still works there at least part of every day. Her children are grown and have long had lives of their own. The family room is filled now not only with Mrs. Wells's sewing materials, but also with toys for her three young grandchildren.

Since 1985, when she first showed her quilts in nearby Northport at the Kentuck Festival of the Arts, Yvonne has acquired an agent, Tuscaloosa folk art dealer Robert Cargo, and a legion of fans.

Her work has been exhibited in a number of prestigious galleries and museums, including the Museum of American Folk Art in New York City. She was among a group of folk artists invited to craft a panel for the skirt wrapped around the 1993 White House Christmas tree. Mrs. Wells also made a heart-shaped ornament that decorated the tree.

Her art is defined by what she calls "the three H's—what the head sees, what the heart feels, and what the hand can create. Put it all together, and you have Yvonne Wells, artist."

208

The Dream, *1993.*
Cotton and cotton blends, buttons, mattress ticking. Dimensions: 88" x 65".
Artist's Collection.

YVONNE WELLS

210

Proverbs, *ca. 1989.*
Cotton, cotton blends, synthetics, buttons. Dimensions: 75" x 63".
Birmingham Museum of Art, Birmingham, Alabama.

Coming Home, 1987.
Cotton blends, buttons. Dimensions: 54" x 83".
Private Collection.

MYRTICE WEST

Born September 14, 1923, in Cherokee County, Alabama
Lives in Centre

One Sunday morning in the late 1970s, Myrtice West headed off for services at her country church in Cherokee County, Alabama. She doesn't know what happened on the way, but when she came to her senses, she was in an unfamiliar little sanctuary, standing at the pulpit, preaching about the Biblical Book of Revelation.

"I'd never been in this church in my life, and there I was, standing up in that pulpit, reading the Bible, and it was open to Revelations. When I come to myself, I said, 'I'm sorry. I don't know what came over me.' One of the women sat up in her pew and said, 'I know her, she's a good Christian, and she draws sometimes, and I bet she can put all that on canvas.' "

Perplexed, Mrs. West got in her car and drove home. For the next few months, she thought about what had happened and what that woman in the congregation had said. She decided that perhaps God was trying to tell her something.

So Myrtice West took an old slipcover, turned it inside out, stretched it like a canvas across a rickety window frame, and sat down to begin painting the Book of Revelation. Seven years later, with 14 oil paintings on wood and canvas lining her hallway, she had finished.

She believes those paintings, and the other Biblically inspired pieces that followed, kept her from losing her sanity during a trying time. "This was something God give me to ease my mind," she says. "If it hadn't been for God givin' me this, I'd be nuttier than a fruitcake."

The Revelations paintings weren't Mrs. West's first attempts at art. As a child, she says, "I always fooled with pictures, cut pictures out of books, drawed them." She made crepe paper flowers, quilted, and did embroidery. Later, she would concentrate on painting happy scenes of flowers, riverboats, southern belles, and her favorite politician, former Alabama governor George Wallace.

But those simple paintings barely resemble the large and complex Biblical pieces she began producing in the late 1970s. Each painting required months of Bible study. Myrtice took a pencil and painstakingly sketched out each scene before putting paint to canvas.

Her dreams and visions influenced the work almost as much as her Bible study did. But, more than anything else, it was the pain and sorrow of seeing her only daughter abused and then murdered that ignited Myrtice West's extraordinary artistic vision.

Born and reared in the small farm towns of Cherokee County, young Myrtice Snead spent more time working in the cotton fields than she did in school. At age 17, when she quit school to marry sharecropper Wallace West, Myrtice had only an eighth-grade education.

While her new husband, an enlisted man, was stationed overseas during World War II, she toiled in her father's cotton fields.

When Wallace West returned to Centre in the mid-1940s, he and Myrtice moved to Atlanta, where he took a job in a factory. During the long days alone at home, Myrtice dreamed of being mother to a houseful of children. After two miscarriages she took to her bed in a deep depression.

When she finally summoned the strength to get up, she decided her childhood hobby of art might help ease her mind. So she sat on her bedroom floor with pencils, paints, and paper. "All I wanted to do was draw pictures of Jesus," she recalls. "It just seemed like the end of the world, like nothing was worth

Myrtice West   8/29/93 Centre, Alabama

nothing. I'd lay down on the floor and draw pictures of Christ, over and over, just pictures of Christ." In the mid-1950s, after doctors discovered and removed a cancerous stomach tumor, Myrtice gave birth to a daughter, Martha Jane.

The family moved back to Centre, where the Wests ran a small printing company. Wallace West also got interested in photography and eventually found work photographing weddings and other family events. Myrtice, who served as his assistant, enrolled in a correspondence course to learn how to hand tint black-and-white photographs.

When Martha Jane entered high school, Myrtice West decided it was time to resume her own education. Enrolling in adult education classes, she told her daughter that she would complete her high school education by the time Martha Jane graduated. "I got so nervous taking that GED test," Mrs. West recalls. "But I passed, and I came home and said, 'I told you I'd do it.'"

Although mother and daughter were close, Martha Jane didn't listen to Myrtice's protests when, at age 15, she married her high school sweetheart, Brett Barnett. Even before the two married, Mrs. West had glimpsed Barnett's violent temper. After the wedding Barnett's rages grew worse, and he began striking his young wife, even hitting her in the stomach during her two pregnancies.

In 1977, Barnett, who had joined the air force, announced he would soon be stationed in Japan and planned to move his family there. After they left, Myrtice painted yet another portrait of Jesus dressed in brilliant blue robes and descending from the clouds.

"I had the feeling Martha Jane and the babies might not live to come back, because of him [Barnett]," Myrtice recalls. She did that portrait of Christ in blue for them, and especially for her young grandson.

That painting became the first in her Revelations series, spurred on by that peculiar Sunday morning visit to the little country church, where she found herself preaching to the congregation of strangers. Back home, she began her study of Revelations and finally tried putting her thoughts onto canvas.

"It seemed like [the prophet] John was putting these pictures in my mind, telling me the colors to use and everything. It just kept pestering me 'til I set down and tried it."

As Myrtice got deeper into the project, Martha Jane and her family moved back to the states, settling for a while in Cherokee County. Brett Barnett's abuse, Mrs. West learned, not only hadn't stopped but also had grown to include her grandson.

Young and naive, Martha Jane had lived with her husband for nearly a decade when she finally decided she'd had enough. In the mid-1980s she left her husband and moved with her children to Birmingham.

But Myrtice's nightmare soon played itself out. During a gathering in Centre to celebrate their daughter's birthday, Brett Barnett beat Martha Jane with a belt and then shot her five times, in front of her stunned family.

That he is now in an Alabama prison, serving a life sentence for Martha Jane's murder, is of little comfort to the Wests. After burying their only child, they were left to care for their two traumatized grandchildren. The older one, Bram, is away at school in North Carolina. The younger child, Kara, a precocious teenager, lives with her grandparents and attends school in Centre.

Money, never in plentiful supply for the Wests, has been particularly scarce in recent years. Wallace West was diagnosed with cancer years ago and has long been unable to work. To supplement their Social Security checks, Myrtice sells her paintings and takes care of an elderly

Ezekiel Visions #4, *1993.*
Oil on canvas. Dimensions: 39" x 47".
Rising Fawn Folk Art Gallery, Lookout Mountain, Tennessee.

boarder. Myrtice's 90-year-old mother is also a resident in their old bungalow.

Dressed in pink polyester pants, a flowery blouse, green-and-yellow argyle socks, and brown sandals, Mrs. West sits in a swing on her front porch, which is decorated by a life-sized painting of Jesus. Hanging from the porch ceiling are her wooden angel cutouts, inspired by a visit with artist Howard Finster in nearby Summerville, Georgia.

Since her daughter's death in 1986, Myrtice has completed a second set of Revelations paintings and has started illustrating the Book of Ezekiel. Life has been better lately, she says. But when sickness hits or the bills pile up or the memories come flooding back, she gets out her paints and brushes and goes to work.

"When I get so much on me I can't get no further," she says, "I just paint."

216

Return of Christ in the Spirit to All Churches *(Revelations series), 1978.*
Oil on reverse vinyl upholstery. Dimensions: 42" x 33 3/4".
Artist's Collection.

MYRTICE WEST

Christ Opening the Book to the Entire World *(Revelations series), 1980.*
Oil on reverse vinyl upholstery. Dimensions: 32" x 52 1/2".
Artist's Collection.

666—Satan on Earth *(Revelations series)*, 1981.
Oil on plywood, painted on both sides. Dimensions: 31" x 42 ½".
Artist's Collection.

MARY WHITFIELD

Born April 14, 1947, in Birmingham, Alabama
Lives in Great Neck, Long Island, New York

lthough Mary Whitfield grew up and still lives in the New York City area, her art is rooted firmly in the Deep South. When she brushes the watercolor paints onto the canvas board, the images that appear evoke the old Confederacy, when slavery and suffering were the rituals of black plantation life.

"I don't know where this comes from, to tell you the truth," says the artist, sitting at the dining room table in her aunt's home in Birmingham, Alabama. "It's almost like I lived there, like I've been reincarnated."

She disappears into a bedroom and returns with one of her most recent paintings. Called "Mary," it depicts a black girl hanging by her neck from a tree in a cemetery full of dead slaves. An old man, who has come with his shovel to bury the girl, has fallen to his knees, overcome with grief.

The painting is done in shades of brown and green, except for the white of the gravestones, the rope and the dead girl's dress. The image is both startling and haunting. That the artist named the dead girl after herself suggests she, too, has suffered.

"I imagine the white stands for purity," Mrs. Whitfield says, looking at the picture. "I decided she had run away more than one time, and this was her punishment. The old man has a shovel, but it's hard for him to dig the grave. He's in a lot of grief, especially with her being a young girl."

"I named her Mary because of myself. Certain injustices I've felt, if you want me to be very honest. I think black people are still second-class citizens. We have a lot of opportunities, it's true. I've had three boys in college. But once you get to where you want to go, it's almost like you're a spectator there."

"I show my grief in my art. Instead of verbally saying things, I work it out in my paintings."

Born in Birmingham on the eve of the civil rights movement, Mary spent her early years in the care of her grandmother. Her mother and father had separated, and her mother eventually headed for New York to work as housekeeper.

Mary still has vivid memories of her years in Alabama, when her grandmother began to get involved in the burgeoning fight for racial equality. "She'd take me to those meetings at night, and I'd be so frightened," Mrs. Whitfield recalls. "She wasn't scared, but I sure was.

"I remember that we went to church all the time, too, the Church of Christ. My grandmother loved going to church."

Mary often visited her mother in New York, staying for long stretches and then returning to Birmingham. When her mother remarried, Mary went to live with her mother and stepfather in a mostly white neighborhood in Queens, New York.

"I used to cry all the time, I felt so out of place," recalls Mrs. Whitfield, who was in the seventh grade when she left Alabama for good. "In junior high, they had a dance, and a white boy asked me to dance. I just couldn't do it. I couldn't even imagine doing it. You didn't do that in Alabama."

Christened Mary Frances Dimples Latham, Mary was known as Dimples throughout her childhood in Birmingham. In New York, however, her new teachers told her the name sounded silly, so she dropped Dimples to become the more serious-sounding Mary.

After she was graduated from high school, Mary married a hardware store salesman named David Whitfield and settled in Great Neck, Long Island, to raise her three boys.

Mary Whitfield   1/24/94 Birmingham, Alabama

She first started painting in the early 1970s, when her two older sons were toddlers. She longed for something to do that was more stimulating than changing diapers and cooking supper. "I was a housewife and lonely," she says. "What's left to do after you clean up?"

Although she had no training in art, Mary was talented at both knitting and embroidery, and she thought she might have a knack for painting. So she rummaged through the garage until she found some old house paint and some pieces of plywood.

She painted the images that came into her head. One of her first pictures, which hangs in her aunt's home in Birmingham, is called "God Bless Our House." It depicts a loving family gathered together in their kitchen.

She enjoyed the hobby, but soon gave it up to enroll in business school. After graduation, she went to work as a secretary for a trade publications company, where, during the last 13 years, she worked her way up to her current position as supervisor of library services.

In 1990, after her children were grown and she again had too much free time, Mary Whitfield bought some watercolor paints and canvas board and resumed her painting career.

Drawing from the wealth of stories told to her as a child by her grandmother, Mary created scenes of the Old South—of black people picking cotton in the fields, of muddy creek baptisms, of washwomen hanging sheets up to dry, and of girls being sold into slavery.

She showed her pictures to her coworkers, who were astonished by her artistic talent and storytelling ability. After seeing an exhibit featuring black artists at her local library, Mary joined the Long Island Black Artists Association and began showing her work to the public.

"A lot of black people are offended by my pictures," she says. "They say they don't want to go back to those days. But I look at it as history, and I love everybody's history."

With help from a Long Island art gallery owner named Phyllis Stigliano, Mrs. Whitfield has been selling her work for as much as $2,000 per painting.

She realizes now that her primitive style, which once made her feel amateurish and untalented, is one of the things that makes her paintings special. "I used to think I wasn't very good. I'd say, 'This looks so elementary.'

"But my boys said to me, 'Mom, that's your technique. It has nothing to do with you painting like Picasso. This is you.' And that's what got me out there."

Barn Dance, *1991.*
Watercolor on canvas board. Dimensions: 16" x 20".
Collection of Rena Selfe.

224

Mary, *1993.*
Watercolor on canvas board. Dimensions 16" x 20".
Artist's Collection.